ILLUSTRATED GUIDE TO

ANCIENT MONUMENTS

These Monuments are held in trust for the nation
by the Secretary of State for Scotland and cared for
on his behalf by the Ministry of Public Building
and Works

Volume VI
SCOTLAND

BY

STUART PIGGOTT, D.Litt., F.B.A., F.S.A.
Abercromby Professor of Prehistoric Archaeology,
University of Edinburgh

and

the late W. DOUGLAS SIMPSON, C.B.E., M.A., Litt.D.,
F.S.A., Hon.F.R.I.A.S.

EDINBURGH
HER MAJESTY'S STATIONERY OFFICE
1970

ANCIENT MONUMENTS SCOTLAND

Purchasers will appreciate that circumstances may arise at any time necessitating alteration to the Hours of Opening, Admission Fees, etc., stated in this Guide Book. A list showing such amendments may be had free on application to Ministry of Public Building and Works (Stationery Section), Argyle House, 3 Lady Lawson Street, Edinburgh EH3 9SD.

SBN 11 490294 1

CONTENTS

NOTE

The Prehistoric Monuments
by Professor Stuart Piggott.

The Roman Occupation and Middle Ages
by the late Dr. W. Douglas Simpson.

This series of Guides to Ancient Monuments
in the care of the Ministry of Public Building
and Works has been planned to cover England,
Wales and Scotland in six volumes.

GLOSSARY

AMBULATORY . .	Covered walk or walk round within a building.
APSE . . .	Circular or polygonal termination of a chancel, chapel or aisle.
ASHLAR . . .	Dressed, squared, masonry.
AUMBRY. . .	Small cupboard within thickness of wall.
BARMKIN . .	Fortified enclosure (Scottish).
BARBICAN . .	Forework for the defence of a castle entrance.
BROACH SPIRE .	A type of spire which rises from the sides of its tower without a parapet.
CELLARIUM . .	Western range of a monastic establishment; containing stores and cellars.
CAP-HOUSE . .	Small chamber at the top of a wheel or spiral stair leading to the open wall-walk of a tower.
CHI-RHO . .	The first two letters of the Greek word for Christ—"the anointed"; used as a sacred monogram in Early Christian times, becoming common in the second quarter of the fourth century.
CORBEL . . .	A projecting stone for the support of a timber beam or overhanging wall.
DONJON . .	The strongest tower of a medieval castle.
DORTER . . .	Monastic dormitory.
ENCEINTE . .	Fortified enclosure.
ENTABLATURE . .	In architecture; the upper part of the classical orders; the architrave, frieze and cornice.
FRATER . . .	Refectory: the monastic dining hall.
GARTH . . .	The cloister garth: the cloister garden.
GROIN VAULT . .	A Gothic vault without ribs.
GUN-LOOP . .	Aperture for gun barrel.
HAMMER-BEAM ROOF	A type of massive open timber roof.
MORAINE . .	Débris deposited by a glacier.
MOTTE . . .	A mound, partly or wholly artificial, upon which a timber castle and palisade was erected in Norman times.
PEND . . .	Vaulted passage (Scottish).
PENNANULAR . .	Forming an incomplete circle.
PILASTER BUTTRESS .	Buttress with slight projection.
PLEASANCE . .	Walled garden of mansion or castle (Scottish).
PORTCULLIS . .	Iron grille raised and lowered in grooves to defend a castle entrance.
PULPITUM . .	Stone screen across east end of nave of church.
QUERN . . .	Hand-mill for grinding corn.
RAVELIN. . .	In fortification; a detached triangular defence-work.
RIB-VAULT . .	A Gothic vault with a structural framework of stone ribs.

ROOD SCREEN . .	A wood or stone screen between nave and choir on which was a "rood" or crucifix.
RUNES . . .	An alphabetical script used by the Vikings.
SACRAMENT HOUSE .	A cupboard or aumbry in a church; used for the reservation of the Host.
SOLAR . . .	An upper hall in a medieval castle or manor-house.
SQUINCH ARCH .	An arch built across an angle.
TRACERY . .	Ornamental stone-work in the upper part of Gothic windows.
TRANSEPTS . .	The northern and southern projecting arms of a cross-shaped medieval church.
TRIBUNE. . .	Dais for a bishop's throne in the apse of a church.
TROMPES . .	See Squinch Arch.
TUMULUS . .	Burial mound.
UNICAMERAL . .	Single-chambered.
VOUSSOIR . .	An arch stone.
YETT . . .	Open iron-work hinged gate or grille (Scottish).
MESOLITHIC (MIDDLE STONE) AGE	Begins about 4000 B.C. in Scotland.
NEOLITHIC (NEW STONE) AGE	Begins about 3000 B.C. in Scotland.
EARLY BRONZE AGE	Begins about 1800 B.C. "Beaker" folk invasions; first general use of metal.
MIDDLE BRONZE AGE	Begins about 1450 B.C.
LATE BRONZE AGE .	Begins about 850 B.C.
IRON AGE . .	Begins in Scotland, about fifth century B.C. and continues into the early Christian era.
ROMAN OCCUPATION OF SCOTLAND	Approximately 80 A.D. until end of second century.
EARLY CHRISTIAN PERIOD	Approximately fifth–eleventh centuries A.D.
THE MIDDLE AGES .	Approximately eleventh–sixteenth centuries A.D.
ROMANESQUE OR NORMAN ARCHITECTURE	Approximately twelfth century.
GOTHIC ARCHITECTURE	Approximately thirteenth-fifteenth centuries.
"DECORATED" STYLE	A Gothic style of the fourteenth century.
"FLAMBOYANT" STYLE	Late Gothic style characterised by flame-like curves in window tracery.

LIST OF ILLUSTRATIONS

THE PREHISTORIC MONUMENTS:
THE PHYSICAL BACKGROUND

For an understanding of the distribution and the original natural setting of the prehistoric monuments described in this Guide, a recognition of two factors is necessary. In the first place the monuments now in the charge of the Minister under the provisions of the Ancient Monuments Acts which form the subject-matter of the Guide do not, for the prehistoric period at least, give a fair picture of the geographical distribution of the ancient human population of Scotland over the period *c.* 3000 B.C. to the early centuries A.D. which brought them into being, nor are they representative of all the phases of culture over that time. They have in the past largely been selected as striking examples of structures comprehensible to the public as pieces of primitive architecture, with a result that stone-built tombs or domestic sites predominate. The less monumental structures in, for instance, earthwork construction, or the now invisible sites of timber-built settlements, burials and hoards or single finds of metal or pottery, are necessarily unrepresented, although on these much of the structure of Scottish prehistory is based. And within the monuments, selection in the past has not always been based on the scientific principles of providing a representative sample throughout the prehistoric period, and over the whole of Scotland.

The second factor to be taken into account demands longer discussion. The fact that the monuments were built by man implies at once his presence and his activities in the areas of their occurrence, so that we are dealing from the first with man in his natural environment. Never a passive agent in the landscape, from the beginning of the third millennium B.C. to the present day prehistoric, historic and modern man has been to a greater or lesser degree altering his environment in Scotland as elsewhere, and even on much of the moorland and high grass pastures we are looking at a man-made and not a natural landscape. But the formation of this has taken five thousand years, and in antiquity the natural environment was highly significant in determining the areas of colonisation or settlement, the routes of movement or of trade, or the regions of agriculture and pasturage. We must turn to the physical geography of ancient Scotland, its plant cover, and its natural resources in food and minerals.

9

A generation ago there was a tendency towards a modified geographical determinism in British prehistory, and Scotland, as a part of a "Highland Zone" of Britain, was relegated to a position in which its prehistoric populations hardly did more than acquire, late and at second hand, technological or social innovations originating in a "Lowland Zone" of southern and eastern England. A detached re-assessment of the evidence, rather than any emotive rejection of such a thesis north of the Border, has in fact shown it to be in large measure untenable, but this does not obscure two facts. In the first place the natural environment of man in Scotland is conditioned by the fact that the subsoil is that of geologically ancient rocks, in common with other areas of western and northern Britain, and in the second, Scotland, and still more the Orkney and Shetland Islands, form the northernmost part of Britain, itself an island set off the north-west coast of continental Europe in latitudes which also cross the Scandinavian countries: Kirkwall in Orkney matches up with Uppsala in Sweden; Edinburgh with Copenhagen. The Orkneys are as near the Arctic Circle as they are to London, and the Shetlands are on the same latitude as Bergen and Helsinki. Like Scandinavia then, Scotland in ancient times was a northern peripheral outpost of Europe, far from the mainstream of cultural change.

Scotland itself, by geography and tradition, is divided into Highlands and Lowlands. North and west of the line of the Great Fault from the Clyde to the east coast near Stonehaven, lie the largely mountainous tracts of the Highlands, with a deeply indented western coastline and the Islands lying beyond. Much of the main massif was never inhabited, from the earliest antiquity up to today, but there is good open country around the Moray Firth and, in less favourable climatic conditions, in Caithness, while fertile valleys run into the mountains from the east and, partly as sea lochs, on the west. Sea communications are more effective than land routes in the west, while in the Hebrides the repellent nature of their eastern coasts, and the potentially good farming lands on the *machair* areas to the west, led to movements of settlement and trade along the Atlantic shores. To the north, the comparative remoteness and difficulty of access of the Orkney and Shetland Islands did not deter colonists from at least the later third millennium B.C. and perhaps earlier, but the isolation of the islands also led to the long survival of traditions once established.

South of the Clyde, miniature "Highland" conditions are reproduced in Galloway, with much evidence of prehistoric settlement from the earliest known traces of man in Scotland, *c.* 4000 B.C., but the main areas of early occupation in the Lowlands are in the Border counties such as Peebleshire, Roxburghshire and Berwickshire, and again northwards in Fife and Perthshire and up the east coast plains which north of the Dee and Don join with the Moray Firth region already mentioned: from Perthshire onwards human settlement dates from at least the early third millennium B.C.

Over much of these inhabited regions the natural vegetation before its modification by the first agriculturalists would have been woodland, predominantly the characteristic North European deciduous mixed-oak forest. The oak was not everywhere the dominant forest tree, and some comparatively unmountainous areas (such as Caithness and parts of Sutherland) may have been largely open country approximating to a steppe environment: the evidence for wild horses here, probably in the later third millennium B.C., might be significant in this respect. The Orkneys and Shetlands must have had little if any forest cover at the time of their first settlement probably at the end of the third millennium, nor could there have been much in the Outer Hebrides. Stone was often used as a substitute for timber in house construction, and an alternative source was drift wood, some of which in Shetland in the middle second millennium, and there and in North Uist in the early centuries of the Christian era, had floated in ocean currents from North America. But the forests were not the only plant resources used by early man: edible nuts, roots and fruit as well as the seeds of wild plants made into porridge or gruel all offered a complementary item of diet side-by-side with the protein intake from meat and fish.

Here the natural resources were considerable. Red deer are forest dwellers in natural conditions and reindeer could have survived in the extreme north; wild cattle and pigs are indigenous to the deciduous forest zone, and the rivers and coasts would not only provide fish, but the sea mammals. And not only food is involved: before the introduction of domesticated sheep and the use of their wool for fabric, skins alone were available for clothes, and continued to be used for centuries after textile weaving had been achieved. Fur coats have long been status symbols.

For the earliest inhabitants, living by hunting and food-gathering, stone, flint, bone, antler and wood formed the raw material for tools and weapons and this applied also to the first agricultural colonists from soon after 3000 B.C. A millennium later, when copper and gold working was adopted as a novel technology, introduced from outside by new people, there were some Scottish deposits of both metals, but once the copper and tin alloy of bronze had become standard a few centuries later, demands for the rare metal tin, and for increased supplies of copper, must have involved trade, in the first instance as far away as Cornwall, or to North Europe for Bohemian metal. By the fifth century B.C. a knowledge of iron working had been acquired in Scotland, and the local deposits in bogs and elsewhere could be utilised.

So far as climate was concerned, by the time of the first human inhabitants in Scotland the relatively warm and moist Atlantic phase was drawing to a close, to be followed from about 3000 to 1500 B.C. by a warmer and drier Sub-Boreal. It is not perhaps chance that it is from around 3000 B.C. that Britain was first colonised by agriculturalists from continental Europe, nor that at a time probably towards the end of the Sub-Boreal phase we have evidence of barley being grown in regular corn-plots around stone-built houses in Shetland. The climatic deterioration which set in after the middle of the second millennium B.C. may well have resulted in significant changes in the population pattern of early Scotland, and we can even suspect depopulation of some regions.

THE CHRONOLOGICAL BACKGROUND

Prehistory is by definition concerned with the past of man before written records, and although in the Old World writing was coming into use in Mesopotamia by about 3000 B.C., so far as Britain is concerned history conventionally begins with the Roman Conquest of A.D. 43, and in Scotland with Agricola's campaigns of A.D. 80. Before the first century A.D. there are of course incidental references to Britain, as there are to other barbarian peoples beyond the bounds of the Roman Empire, and on the other hand the strictly historical evidence for Roman Britain can only be understood with the help of a considerable degree of archaeological reinforcement. Furthermore, in Scotland in particular, Romanisation amounted only to the establishment of a military garrison, with its communication-system, in a limited geographical area, with indigenous prehistoric communities continuing to flourish beyond the military zone, and indeed to a large extent within it as well.

The absence of written records imposes two acute disabilities on the prehistorian. In the first place, without writing there can be no recorded dates for events or periods of time; in the second, there can similarly be no knowledge of the names of peoples or of individuals. The world of prehistory is an anonymous world. The first problem has been exercising the minds of scholars for over a century, and various solutions have been put forward over that time. The most popular but by no means the most satisfactory was also the oldest—to divide the prehistoric past into periods in terms of the substances used to make edge-tools and weapons. This conceptual model of the past defined a Stone "Age", later subdivided into an Old Stone Age (or Palaeolithic period), a Middle Stone Age (Mesolithic) and a New Stone Age (Neolithic), which was followed by a Bronze Age and an Iron Age, the last bringing ancient technology into the historic period. This sequence could be checked in stratified deposits, both natural and man-made, and shown to have a broad validity in at least north-west Europe (where the scheme was invented), and so gave a very simplified chronological sequence without dates, with its beginnings in geological antiquity and its end on the threshold of history. But not only was it a scheme without dates, but it was really only a statement about one branch of ancient technological development in specific areas and in very simplified terms.

Real dating, comparable with but not identical to historical dating in solar years, was brought to prehistory, as to geology, by an increasing understanding of the processes of radio-active disintegration or decay in natural substances. One of these methods of isotopic dating, depending on the rate of decay of a radio-active isotope of carbon with an atomic weight of 14 rather than the normal 12, has enabled a time-scale for prehistory to be constructed, and is referred to as the C_{14} or radiocarbon method. The dates so given are not precise points in time, but a statistical expression of probability within a restricted range, and recent research has shown that radiocarbon "years" are not necessarily at all times in the past the exact equivalents of solar years. With these reservations the cumulative probability established by a large series of C_{14} determinations has given us a time-scale within which we can set the activities of the anonymous communities of prehistoric Scotland as elsewhere.

This brings us to our second problem, that of naming groups of peoples for whom no name has survived. The working hypothesis employed by prehistorians is that a recurrent pattern of material products (types of houses, tombs, pots, axes), particularly when taken with the evidence for subsistence (hunting and food-gathering as against agriculture for instance) should be interpreted as indicating a social unit such as might be recognised as a distinctive tribe or other well-defined group in non-industrialised societies. To these assemblages of material remains, which constitute archaeological evidence, the prehistorian applies the term "culture". Where our evidence does not permit of precision we still may have to fall back on the old Stone-Bronze-Iron terminology, but with some refinements: Neolithic cultures we can now see as those of the first stone-using agri-culturalists, Mesolithic comprising the latest hunter-fishers; for Britain the Bronze Age roughly lies within a time-span from early in the second millennium to the middle of the first millennium B.C. Our terminology is haphazard and inelegant, but it is all we have to work with at present, apart from the chronological sequence provided by such means as C_{14} dating.

In this Guide the treatment of the prehistoric monuments will be within the framework of C_{14} chronology and cultural classifications will be avoided as much as possible, as these rarely have a significance except to prehistorians.

THE THIRD MILLENNIUM: *c.* 3000 to *c.* 2000 B.C.

By a convenient accident, a decisive phase in British prehistory, that marked by the first introduction of a subsistence-economy based not on hunting and gathering, but on mixed farming, seems to have opened around 3000 B.C. For a thousand years or so, stone-using agriculturalists developed variant regional "Neolithic" cultures in the British Isles until, when these cultures were still flourishing in the centuries immediately after 2000 B.C., new immigrants appeared who introduced and rapidly developed the working of copper and gold, and soon the by now mixed population included metal-smiths skilled in the copper-tin alloy of bronze. The third millennium B.C. then more or less contains the cultures denoted "Neolithic" in the old scheme, although many stone-using communities must have continued their way of life untouched for centuries after technical innovations had been introduced and adopted in other areas. This was certainly the case in the Orkneys and Shetland, and probably in other areas of mainland Scotland in the north and west.

The final insulation of Britain from the Continent, with the formation of the English Channel, seems to have taken place in the Late Boreal climatic phase about 6000 B.C. As we have seen, a warmer, moister, period set in, the Atlantic phase, from about 5000 B.C., with the development of deciduous forest cover: in this phase we have the earliest known evidence of man in Scotland in the form of temporary camp sites marked by a scatter of flint implements and the debris of their manufacture, one such site being recently dated to *c.* 4000 B.C. The total population of these hunting and fishing groups of Mesolithic peoples in Britain must have been tiny by modern standards, perhaps no more than 10,000 persons all told, and in Scotland their culture survived until the appearance of agriculturalists in the Forth Estuary and on the west coast at least, until about 3000 B.C. The Mesolithic contributions to subsequent technology included the use of boats: island settlements such as Risga or Oransay, and the presence in their food debris of the bones of fish only obtainable by deep-water fishing demand the use of boats, either hollowed from a split tree-trunk or of skins stretched on a wooden frame in the manner of the Eskimo umiak or the Irish curragh.

The appearance of peoples growing cereal crops of wheat and barley and having flocks of domesticated sheep, goats, pigs and cattle, can, in

Scotland as elsewhere in Britain, only be the result of the arrival of immigrants by sea from the European continent. The grasses ancestral to wheat and barley do not grow wild in Britain, nor indeed in western Europe, and the same applies to wild sheep and goats: the so-called wild goats of the Highlands are domesticated stock reverted to feral conditions, and the St. Kilda and Shetland sheep represent early man-created breeds. Using the archaeological evidence supported by C_{14} dating we can trace the spread of agriculture from the Near East into south-east Europe by about 6000 B.C.; to central Europe a couple of millennia later, and to north-west continental Europe and the British Isles by about 3000 B.C. And one of the most interesting results from our own radiocarbon dates is to show that instead of the slow spread of agriculture from the Channel coasts to the Pentland Firth that had formerly been visualised, the Neolithic settlement of Scotland hardly if at all lagged behind that of the rest of Britain—just around 3000 B.C. in the Isle of Arran and about 2800 B.C. at Pitnacree in Perthshire for instance—and in keeping with a whole series of dates within this range from Ireland, south and north England, and Wales. Not only have we the evidence from actual settlements and burial monuments, but the influence of agriculturalists in clearing forests and tilling land can be detected in the disturbances in the natural vegetation sequence provided by pollen grains in stratified peat or sediment deposits at this same time. In terms of plant history and the climatic changes they reflect, this as we saw marks the beginning of the Sub-Boreal period, with temperatures probably about 2°C. higher than the modern average, and with less precipitation than in the Atlantic phase. The two events, the climatic improvement and the introduction to north-west Europe, dated to the beginning of the third millennium, may well not be unconnected.

All recent research has shown in an increasing degree the complexity of the immigrant movements which laid the foundations of the British Neolithic cultures, and indeed those in which bronze and iron were used. Nowhere is this better demonstrated than in the monumental funerary architecture of the collective stone-chambered tombs which form the bulk of the monuments in the Minister's care which can be assigned to the third millennium B.C. in Scotland. Of some 20 sites certainly or probably of this date there are 10 chambered tombs in the Orkneys and others are scattered in Arran, Argyll, Bute, Caithness, Kirkcudbrightshire, Inverness-shire, Ross and Cromarty, and Sutherland. The total number of chambered tombs in Scotland is something over 400, and the Orkney tombs largely represent highly individual architectural solutions to the basic problem of providing a burial monument to certain ritual requirements, developing in isolation from the main streams of culture at the time, but elsewhere representatives of these central architectural traditions current in such monuments can be seen. Collective chambered tombs form an archaeological phenomenon, and a problem, which is not confined to Scotland nor to the British Isles, but is common to many areas of western and north-western Europe. We must look very briefly at this problem as a whole before turning to the monuments which represent it.

In Iberia, the British Isles, the Low Countries and the North European plain, and in southern Scandinavia there exist an enormous number— perhaps 40,000–50,000—of monumental stone-built tombs normally for the collective burial of several persons, and the association of these with archaeological material in the form of grave-offerings, and the evidence of radiocarbon dating, show these in the main to date from the third millennium B.C., with a few rather earlier than this and some certainly belonging to the second millennium. Wherever they appear they are associated with early stone-using agriculturalists in the various regions of their distribution, and they show a remarkable consistent conformity to two or three main architectural traditions of planning and construction over the very wide area where they occur. Two main problems are raised: was there a spread from a single centre of origin, and by what means, in terms of the actual activities of human beings, was the tradition propagated? Fortunately we do not have to answer these questions here, and we need only say that the older thesis of a vaguely Mediterranean origin for the whole chambered tomb tradition is now seen to be virtually impossible to support, and that local origins for specific types are by no means excluded: on C_{14} dating the earliest known tombs are in west France. To this we may add that what was involved in the dissemination of such tombs was an architectural tradition reflecting the ritual necessities of formalised funeral rites embodied in some consistent body of belief about the other world, and not the transmission of the tomb type as a part of a wider range of cultural traits. The tombs, and their inferred ritual, are intrusive into the British Isles, but the grave-offerings represent already indigenous cultures. It is worth while remembering that the introduction of Christianity, and the building of churches for the first time in an area, need not, and probably would not, alter the style of table ware or of cutlery.

So far as Britain is concerned, two main architectural traditions can be seen, representative of a duality also present in our earliest agricultural communities. From easterly sources including the North European plain seems to come the tradition of burial under elongated mounds often of formal trapezoid plan; from the westerly Atlantic coasts of Europe the stone-built burial chamber with approach passage under a round mound, the Passage Grave as usually understood. Together with these traditions, we must allow for the intermittent appearance of simple box-like chambers which may be of local origin. The traditions mixed, with consequent hybrid structures, as we shall see. Unfortunately we have so few radio-carbon dates from these tombs in Britain that we are uncertain about possible priorities, but we know that collective stone-built burial chambers in long trapeze-shaped cairns were being built around 2800 B.C. in southern England, and comparable versions somewhat earlier at Monamor in Bute at least. We do not yet know how early the passage grave in the circular cairn was in the British Isles—Newgrange in Ireland dates from c. 2500 B.C —but such tombs date from before 3000 B.C. in Brittany.

Among the Scottish monuments under review, *Cairn Ban* and *Torrylin* in Arran, *Monamor* in Bute, *Brackley* and *Auchoish* in Argyll, and the *Cairnholy* tombs in Kirkcudbrightshire are good examples of the long cairn, rectangular or trapezoid in plan, containing a more or less rectangular burial chamber at the wider end of the cairn, sometimes approached from a monumental crescentic forecourt, and sometimes divided up into seg-ments by transverse slabs. *Monamor* as we saw has a date around 3000 B.C., and a date early in the third millennium B.C. would be likely for most of these monuments. In the British Isles related tombs lie across the sea in Ireland, and versions of the same basic use of the trapezoid cairn are found to the south in the Severn Estuary and Cotswold areas. When we turn to north-east Scotland, we see in the *Long Cairn of Camster* in Caithness a chamber of "passage grave" type, set in a long cairn and entered from the side, suggesting a hybrid form, and recent excavations in a number of Scottish sites have shown that not infrequently a passage grave tomb in a round cairn was later incorporated in a long cairn: the more northerly parts of Scotland were areas where complex architectural syncretism in tomb building took place. At *Nether Largie South Cairn* in Argyll the converse appears, with a burial chamber of the type normally found in the long cairns of south-west Scotland set in a large round mound.

The passage grave type of collective chambered tomb is widely dis-tributed in Scotland in a number of architectural variants, which become funerary eccentricities in the Orkneys, where their building probably and their use certainly, continued into the second millennium B.C. The simpler, classic, "pan-European" passage grave form is to be seen in such sites as *Rudh' an Dunain* in Skye, the *Cairns of Clava* and that of *Corrimony*, though in the two latter sites a ring of free-standing stones around the cairn are local features not normal to passage graves (though known for example at Newgrange in Ireland). Only two of the *Clava* cairns are passage graves, the others being curious ring-cairns again of a localised type and of unknown affinities. In Kirkcudbrightshire, the *White Cairn of Bargrennan* is a small architecturally degenerate passage grave, in which the structural distinction of chamber and passage has been forgotten. Dating these tombs is very difficult in the absence of radiocarbon evidence and

B

the few archaeological finds, but there were secondary burials in *Rudh' an Dunain* with a Beaker pot of the early second millennium B.C., and pottery from the primary burials was comparable with that from *Nether Largie*, again earlier than a Beaker burial, and so likely to be of the third millennium B.C., though probably not very early in it.

In north-east Scotland and Orkney we find a most interesting situation in the development of the chambered tomb architectural tradition into a series of highly individual and odd forms, and here too for the first time we can link at least the later use of the tombs with contemporary settlement sites. One of our difficulties in interpreting the evidence from these graves, used and re-used over a long period of time, is to decide which grave offerings (if any) belong to the original burials, contemporary with the building of the tomb, and which to later deposits. From the finest passage grave in the Orkneys, and indeed in Britain, *Maes Howe*, we have no such finds, for the tomb was plundered in the twelfth century A.D. by the Vikings, who recorded their visits in a couple of dozen Runic inscriptions and some drawings including a splendidly lively dragon, scratched on the walls of the burial chamber. The stone-built passage and chamber are contained within a huge circular mound 115 feet in diameter, within a broad ditch: the passage is over 30 feet long, the inner part roofed, walled and floored by enormous single slabs averaging over 18 feet long. The chamber is 15 feet square, with a corbelled (or false-vaulted) roof rising originally to some 25 feet above floor level. Three burial compartments open two or three feet above the floor in the side and end walls and these, like the outer passage entrance, were originally closed by massive stone blocks. The whole work, executed in the admirably suitable local Caithness flagstone, has an architectural precision and sophistication virtually unparalleled in the British Isles, and hardly approached anywhere among European tombs of the same type.

Other tombs in Orkney, such as *Wideford Hill, Cuween, and Quoyness*, can be seen to have plans which are increasingly asymmetric and aberrant forms of that of *Maes Howe*, and the tomb on the *Holm of Papa Westray* shows this development in even more eccentric form than Quoyness. Another series of tombs, those of *Taversoe Tuick, Unstan, Yarso, Blackhammer* and *Midhowe*, show again plans increasingly diverging from another prototype, a simple chamber with projecting lateral slabs in a round cairn, as in the *Round Cairn of Camster* in Caithness, and becoming, in the last three Orcadian tombs, enclosed in oval or oblong mounds to accommodate the grotesquely elongated chambers, divided by numbers of side slabs into "stalls" for the various burial deposits: *Papa Westray* is similarly elongated. *Taversoe Tuick* has the further peculiarity of being in two storeys, with one chamber built on the roofing slabs of the other, and the *Dwarfie Stane* on Hoy is a chambered tomb cut in a single rock mass instead of being built of separate stones.

All these architectural vagaries and unorthodox versions of the simple passage grave form recall the parallel development of localised variants in Continental regions such as south-western and western Brittany, where the tradition of chambered tomb building endured for many centuries. In the north Scottish series the beginning is difficult to date but is likely to lie in the third millennium. Pottery which may be considered primary in several tombs with evolved plans, such as Unstan and Taversoe Tuick, is comparable with vessels from a settlement site in Perthshire with C_{14} dates of *c.* 2000 B.C., and other grave-offerings (in some cases certainly secondary) link certain tombs such as Quoyness to the settlement sites of *Skara Brae* and *Rinyo*, which belong to the early and middle second millennium B.C.

The complex monument of *Callanish* in Lewis, which includes a small passage grave within a circle of standing stones with accompanying alignments, is best discussed with other stone circles, which as a body appear to belong to the second millennium. Here too belong the *Skara Brae* settlement in Orkney, the *Stanydale* structure in Shetland, and probably the first phase of the monument on *Cairnpapple Hill* in West Lothian, a cremation cemetery which could be before 2000 B.C. but probably belongs a century or so later.

THE EARLIER SECOND MILLENNIUM:
c. 2000 to *c.* 1400 B.C.

To make a division around 2000 B.C. in British prehistory is not merely to take refuge in a conveniently round number of centuries. Even on the Continent there is a perceptible break in many parts of western and northern Europe towards the end of the third millennium, the archaeological evidence suggesting a severing of old traditions, the shifting of populations, and the appearance of new technological advances, the most important being the adoption, by peoples previously using stone and flint for edge-tools and weapons, of the techniques of non-ferrous metallurgy—the exploitation and working of copper and gold. Copper alloys were soon discovered, giving superior hardness and toughness, either using arsenic or the much more satisfactory tin, forming normal bronze. In the older archaeological terms we are seeing the beginning of "The Bronze Age" in north-western Europe; a technological increment which the agricultural communities of the Near East may have acquired as early as the fifth or sixth millennium, and those in east and east-central Europe certainly by the fourth. In the west, copper-working in Iberia dates from before the middle of the third millennium B.C., and copper objects of east European derivation had been circulating in northern Europe since around 3000 B.C. Much of the copper-working of the west seems however to have involved a widespread group of peoples making the highly characteristic pottery known as Beakers, and Britain was subjected to immigrations, probably on a relatively large scale by prehistoric standards, by such people, during the centuries following 2000 B.C. The opening of the second millennium in British prehistory is then marked by the arrival of newcomers, impinging on the thousand year old traditions of the now indigenous stone-using agriculturalists, and bringing with them the knowledge and skills that could set in motion a minor Industrial Revolution, the beginnings of metal working. The basic pattern of agricultural subsistence seems to have remained unchanged, but the necessity of obtaining metal ores led to the establishment of a network of primitive trade relations on a scale unknown before, although tough stones for axe-blades had been traded throughout the third millennium.

The origin and precise routes of movement of the makers of Beakers on the Continent is a current topic of discussion among prehistorians, but as far as Britain is concerned the situation is reasonably clear: our colonists arrived almost certainly from the Low Countries and the Rhineland soon after 2000 B.C., and their points of entry stretched almost simultaneously from Aberdeenshire to the English Channel, so that northeast Scotland was an area of primary settlement. Originally preserving more or less intact their cultural traditions in pottery-making, metalworking, and single-grave burial as opposed to that in collective tombs, the immigrants merged with the local population before long to form a distinctive series of insular cultures which were an amalgam partly of old and partly of new ideas. With the immigrations of the Beaker people, Britain, which since the centuries around 3000 B.C. had become increasingly out of touch with Continental developments, was brought back into the cultural mainstream of western Europe and, as a result of the trade in copper, gold and tin, remained in touch for five or six centuries, after which insularity (though not technological stagnation) seems once again to have supervened. The monuments in Scotland to which we now turn illustrate various aspects of the mixed cultural traditions just described, particularly interesting being those which show continuity of tradition and conservatism in remote peripheral areas.

Perhaps the best key to the period as a whole is provided by the remarkable series of ceremonial and burial monuments on *Cairnpapple Hill* in West Lothian, which span some five hundred years. The sequence as revealed by excavation comprises four phases within the second millennium, and a fifth probably late in the first. *Cairnpapple I* is represented by the sockets for three massive stones standing like a Greek π in plan, the open end facing an irregular arc of deposits of cremated human bones, some in small pits. Such cemeteries can be dated from after 2000 B.C. and may have continued in use for some centuries, that of the first phase of Stonehenge being a case in point. In *Cairnpapple II* the standing stones were removed and against their site a grave was dug to contain a burial with two Beakers, covered by a very small stone-kerbed mound. This was then eccentrically contained within an oval setting of standing stones, 26 in all, itself within a rock-cut ditch and external bank with opposed entrances to north and south, the whole comprising a ceremonial site of a type well known in Britain as a Henge Monument. Another burial with a Beaker was placed against a stone of the oval setting, and all three vessels probably date from round about 1600 B.C.

Cairnpapple III marks a move from a ceremonial to a purely funerary monument. The oval of standing stones was dismantled (recalling similar dismantling of the contemporary monument of Stonehenge II) and, it seems, re-used prone as kerb-stones of a circular cairn 50 feet in diameter, containing two stone-slabbed burial cists, one very massive and with an offering-vessel of the type known as a Food Vessel. This cairn overlapped two of the sockets of the now removed stone oval of the Henge Monument, and the pot is probably of the fifteenth or sixteenth century B.C. In *Cairnpapple IV* this cairn was enlarged to twice its diameter, now overlapping five more stone-holes of the Henge and a part of its silted-up ditch, and contained two cremation burials in pots of the Cinerary Urn type, probably of the fourteenth century B.C. The sequence of Cairnpapple I–IV forms a convenient chronological and cultural scale against which most of the other monuments now to be discussed can be set.

One of the most remarkable prehistoric sites in Britain, the settlement of stone-built houses at *Skara Brae* in Orkney, is broadly contemporary with Cairnpapple I–II. This village, and a similar site excavated at Rinyo on Rousay, had an occupation spread over more than one building phase, and the dates in the seventeenth and sixteenth century B.C. which most of the pottery and other objects from the site would imply need not be the earliest for the beginning of the occupation: pottery of Skara Brae type from the south of England has recently been given radiocarbon dates of about 1600 B.C. Although by this date not only copper, but tin-bronze, was in use in many areas of Scotland and elsewhere in the British Isles, the inhabitants of Skara Brae were still stone-using pastoralists, breeding cattle and sheep and collecting shell-fish, but leaving no evidence that they grew grain. Remains of eight houses were recovered in that part of the site that had not been destroyed by coastal erosion, buried deep in sand-dunes that had preserved the walls in places to a height of eight feet. Lack of timber and the availability of easily split flagstone resulted in the furniture of the houses—beds and dressers against the walls—being stone-built, and therefore surviving to the present day.

A typical dwelling is a rectangular room with rounded corners some 15 feet to 20 feet square. It was entered through a low, narrow doorway, less than 5 feet high, that could be closed by a stone slab fastened by a bar that slid in bar-holes cut in the stone door jambs. A peat fire burned on a square, kerbed hearth in the middle of the room. On either side enclosures framed by slabs on edge served as beds—naturally lined with heather or hay. Each bed could be covered by a canopy of skins supported by stone bedposts which still survive. Recesses in the wall above it would serve as keeping places for the personal possessions of the bed's occupants. A two-shelved stone dresser was built against the rear wall. Tanks, framed with slate slabs and luted to hold liquids, were let into the floor. Cells in the thickness of the walls may have served as store cupboards or perhaps as privies. Some are served by drains such as run under the floor of every house.

The better to exclude draughts due to the continuous gales, "midden"—ash, dung and rubbish mixed with sand—was piled round the house-walls and kept in place by retaining walls. Eventually all the spaces between the huts were packed with midden, and the alleys joining them were walled and roofed with stone and then also buried in midden. A well-built sewer, which can now be visited by trapdoors, drained the complex. The whole must have looked like a great anthill with crater-like smoke-holes over each dwelling and two or three tunnel-like entries on the flanks. The eastern exit of the main alley has been washed away, but on the west it opened through a door on to a paved area. Beyond this is a single free-standing building. This contains no beds and a kiln instead of a dresser.

The semi-subterranean houses with their arrangement of passage-entrance, beds and hearth, recall types of house which have survived among northern peoples such as the Eskimo until recent times, and represent an adaptation within the Circumpolar Zone to difficult climatic conditions; in Shetland the problem was solved in a different way at much the same time.

The structure at *Stanydale*, Sandsting, which has been called a "temple" is an exceptionally large representative of a class of prehistoric house now known to be widespread in the Shetland Islands but unknown elsewhere: its interpretation as a religious structure is based on assumptions and not evidence that it was a house for deities and not men. It is oval or "heel-shaped" in plan, with very massive thick stone walls and an internal area of some 40 by 20 feet, and had a roof supported on timber uprights, the material for which was drift-wood pine and spruce, the latter of North American origin. The planning of the Stanydale and other houses of its type in the Shetlands appears to be related to that of the local chambered tombs: houses of the dead and houses of the living. Their builders, as we know from several other sites, were prehistoric crofters, growing barley in little stone-cleared plots of irregular outline adjacent to their houses, and with domesticated cattle and sheep, and like the inhabitants of Skara Brae, without knowledge of metals. Their pottery and other objects show them to be in the main contemporary with the later phases of Beaker making, around about 1600 B.C., and contemporary with Cairnpapple II.

This monument, with its standing stones within a ditch and bank, has Orkney counterparts in the Henge Monuments of the *Ring of Brogar* and the *Ring of Stenness*, and similar sites are widely scattered elsewhere in Scotland and England, where C_{14} dates for a double-entrance Henge with pottery comparable to that of Skara Brae show it to be about 1600 B.C., though other types of Henge are earlier. Adjacent to the circle of standing stones at *Loanhead of Daviot* in Aberdeenshire a reduced and simplified version of such a double-entrance enclosure contained a cremation cemetery with a likely date in the first half or middle of the second millennium.

These sites lead us to another class of ceremonial monument, the circles of upright stones without an enclosing bank and ditch. Simple circles of this type are widespread in the British Isles where suitable stones for their construction occur and, like the Henge Monuments, seem to be a distinctively insular development without Continental prototypes. Such circles, such as *Torhouse* in Wigtownshire or *Lamlash* in Arran, are very difficult to date, often even after excavation, but they are probably to be placed in the earlier rather than the later second millennium B.C. A specialised north-east Scottish group, the Recumbent Stone circles, include such examples as *Loanhead of Daviot*, *East Aquhorthies* in Aberdeenshire, or *Glassel* in Kincardineshire, and is characterised by having a large slab horizontally placed between two flanking uprights at one point of the circumference, and a low burial cairn in the centre. They were made or used by makers of Beaker pottery, probably about 1800–1600 B.C., and so again are roughly of the period of Cairnpapple II. They may in some way be related to the Clava ring-cairns with their enclosing stone circles.

At *Callanish* in Lewis is a remarkable monument consisting of a miniature passage grave in a round cairn, eccentrically set within a circle of tall standing stones from which radiate four rows of similar uprights. This site is without parallel, and much has been made of the astronomical significance of its alignments, and of sight-lines which can be made here and from other circles. These claims raise very difficult questions involving the degree of mathematical sophistication likely to exist in ancient barbarian societies, but a standard unit of length, 2·72 feet, does however seem to have been established as current in second millennium Britain, and used in laying out ceremonial monuments.

Apart from the very exceptional settlement sites such as Skara Brae or the Shetland crofts, most of the archaeological evidence for the second millennium comes from burials. The makers of Beaker pottery introduced the burial rite of a single inhumation in a grave, sometimes stone-lined to form a cist, and sometimes under a mound or cairn. Such single-graves are characteristic of the early second millennium in Britain, sometimes provided with a Beaker, or with another, insular, type of pottery, the Food Vessel; other graves have no pottery, and copper or bronze tools and weapons were also on occasion buried with the dead. Such burials were rarely monumental in character, but in the Kilmartin region of Argyll a remarkable group of burial cairns is of exceptional interest.

We have seen that the *South Cairn of Nether Largie* covered a collective chambered tomb, but the *Mid* and *North Cairns* represent the single-grave tradition in massive and monumental form. The *Mid Cairn* covered two burial cists and was originally bounded by a boulder kerb: no burials or grave-offerings survived but one of the cists had its lateral slabs grooved to take the end-stones in a manner suggesting the techniques of the carpenter rather than the mason, and showing that the prototypes of such stone cists must have been plank coffins. A dozen or so similarly constructed cists are known in the Kilmartin region, and exceptional examples occur in Bute and in the Scilly Islands.

The *North Cairn* contains a very massive central cist, the covering stone of which is carved with upwards of ten shallow representations of flat copper or bronze axe-blades, and about forty "cupmarks". Two further axe-heads are carved on the northern end-slab of the cist. The *Ri Cruin* cairn repeats the features of the Mid and North Cairns of Nether Largie, with three massive cists with grooved or rebated jointing, one of which also has carvings of flat metal axe-heads, and an enigmatic rake-like pattern. Carvings of this type are very rare in Britain: in the Kilmartin region there are also lozenge-patterned stones from Badden and Carnbaan, but axe representations only occur elsewhere in a Dorset barrow and at Stonehenge, both probably later in date than the Kilmartin examples, which show axe-blades of early type and should date from before the middle of the second millennium. The three Nether Largie cairns, that at Ri Cruin, the *Kilmartin Glebe cairn*, and other burials with grooved stone cists, together form a "linear cemetery" over three miles long, in the manner of the contemporary linear cemeteries of Wessex. The *Glebe Cairn* has a double kerb of boulders and encloses two large cists which contained burials of the middle of the second millennium, with pottery of Food Vessel type, contemporary with that from Cairnpapple III, a burial in a massive cist in a cairn with a monumental kerb. Finally, at *Temple Wood Kilmartin* is a monument at first sight looking like a massive cist within a free-standing stone circle, but better explicable as a burial cairn of the same general type as those just described, with a kerb of large upright slabs, robbed to its foundations, with some spoil or original cairn material still remaining outside the circle.

The "cup-marks" on the Nether Largie North Cairn, small circular hollows artificially worked on the surface of the stone, lead us to a group of monuments in Argyll and elsewhere in which not only cup-marks, but cups surrounded by one or more circular grooves or rings, have been pecked into the smooth faces of natural rock outcrops. Such cup-and-ring markings are under the care of the Ministry at *Kilmichael Glassary, Achnabreck, Ballygowan, Baluacraig* and *Carnbaan* in the Crinan region and at other sites such as *Drumtroddan* near Port William in Wigtownshire. The significance of these sculptures is unknown, and as with all prehistoric art can never be recovered owing to the lack of written documents to inform us of their makers' beliefs. They have a limited distribution in Scotland and northern England, and can be dated only by reference to similar designs on the stones of cists dating from the first half of the second millennium: cup-marked stones occurred at Cairnpapple in Phase III.

As we have seen, substantially all the monuments so far described have belonged approximately to the period 2000–1500 B.C., or perhaps continuing for a century or so later. More difficult to date are monuments such as the multiple rows of small standing stones at *The Hill O' Many Stanes* and *Cnoc Freicadain* in Caithness, or the single or grouped large standing stones such as those in the Kilmartin region and many sites elsewhere. Some of these may belong to the later second millennium or the early part of the first, for which the archaeological evidence does not on present showing include any demonstrable field monuments, but is virtually confined to objects of metal, and some types of domestic pottery, and some of the cremated burials such as those of Cairnpapple IV, one dated in Perthshire to as late as *c.* 1200 B.C. It is difficult to place any of our second millennium monuments in Scotland more than a century or two after 1500 B.C., and when we take up the story again, we are nearly a thousand years nearer to our own times.

THE LATER FIRST MILLENNIUM B.C. AND BEYOND: *c.* 600 B.C. to A.D. 300

As we saw, so far as the field monuments of prehistoric Scotland are concerned, we have a gap, a sort of Dark Age, between those which we may think to be somewhat later than 1400 B.C. or so, and the point at which we next have structural evidence to consider, from about 600 B.C. During this time the archaeological evidence largely consists of bronze tools and weapons, from which we can infer both the development of an accomplished insular tradition of metallurgy, and the incoming and adoption of new types and techniques from the Continent: these European connections are valuable for dating purposes. It was not only tool forms which changed, but methods of warfare, and from early in the first millennium B.C. bronze swords were being made in Scotland to meet the new demands of warriors and eventually, as we shall see, even in the Shetlands. But a new metal technology was soon to supplant bronze for tools and weapons, the working of iron. Knowledge of this new skill was becoming known in Europe north of the Alps by the eighth, and was widespread by the seventh century B.C., and it is interesting to see that the available evidence from Britain suggests that Scotland, as in earlier phases of her prehistory, was not a laggard recipient of the new technology, but acquired it at an early date. Seventh century iron working is known from South Wales, but the technique was hardly established elsewhere until the fifth century, as in Yorkshire, while in Shetland we shall see it could also be of this early date, and certainly is not much later. To return once again to the old terminology, the Iron Age in Scotland is established in some areas at least by the fifth or fourth century B.C., in common with much of the rest of Britain.

In this period too we can for the first time escape from the anonymity of prehistory and recognise an historical people, the Celts, and probably another, the Picts. Forms of the Celtic language must have been current in Europe long before we first hear of the existence of Celtic peoples, around the early sixth century B.C., and the archaeology of Europe north of the Alps before the beginnings of iron working is almost certainly already Celtic archaeology. In what archaeological context we can place the introduction of the earliest Celtic speech into Britain is a matter of active debate, depending on the extent to which we can safely infer actual immigrations of peoples around 500 B.C. from the archaeological evidence. It seems reasonable to suppose however that the appearance of new elements of material culture around this time—pottery forms, fortification techniques, the working of iron—could be equated with the introduction of a new language, known to have been spoken in Britain in the centuries before Caesar or Claudius. This language would have been the P-Celtic Gallo-Brittonic, spoken on both sides of the English Channel, and ancestral to later Welsh, Cornish and Breton. So far as Scotland was concerned, Gallo-Brittonic place and personal names in the classical writers show that the language was spoken as far north as the Orkneys certainly in the first century B.C., and perhaps even in the fourth, and that it was widespread over the country, as in the rest of Britain. It survived into the Middle Ages and beyond not only in place names, but in the Cumbric dialect of Welsh in southern Scotland and north-west England; Gaelic, one need hardly add, is an Irish dialect introduced into Scotland in the fifth century A.D., a Q-Celtic form which in much of western Scotland has come to submerge the older established P-Celtic forms there.

In addition to Celtic, another language, Pictish, must have been current in prehistoric as in early historic times in eastern Scotland, especially in the area between the Forth and the south-east corner of Sutherland. Its structure implies a fusion between a P-Celtic language not identical with Gallo-Brittonic with an indigenous language of unknown, but not Indo-European, affiliations: we will note possible archaeological contexts in which this mixture could happen. The non-Celtic element in Pictish need be one only of many vanished ancient languages in Britain, almost entirely submerged by Gallo-Brittonic but detectable in place names of non-Indo-European forms.

The monuments under consideration, unlike the majority of those of the second millennium, are not sepulchral or ritual, but are settlements and fortifications, and indeed burials of the period are almost unknown in Scotland: the unaccompanied burials of *Cairnpapple V* may be of this date. Forts, of one kind or another, large or small, are characteristic of the Celtic world whether on the Continent or in Britain, and are consistent with the picture of inter-tribal warfare and petty raids among the Celts given by the classical writers from the last couple of centuries B.C., and reflected in the earliest Irish hero-tales, which relate to pre-Christian times. In Scotland, fortifications in part represent types common also to Britain and the Continent, and in part are local specialised developments appearing in response to particular geographical situations and the restriction of the terrain, and probably also to societies organised in smaller units than elsewhere in Britain. This latter class of defended site is best represented by the structures known as brochs, widely distributed over what may be called the Atlantic province of the north and west of Scotland, and including the Hebrides, the Orkneys and Shetland, and sporadically elsewhere; these are in fact defensive tower-houses of circular plan and with ingenious varieties of architectural construction. The settlements frequently took the form of single-house steadings, though hamlets or small villages also existed, and throughout, as with the brochs, we are dealing with dwellings of circular plan in stone (and, as revealed by excavation, in timber as well), although in Shetland the second millennium house-type continued in modified form until at least the fifth century B.C.

The Shetland site on Sumburgh Head known as *Jarlshof* has been excavated to reveal a long series of superimposed prehistoric and early historic dwellings and phases of rebuilding, and the prehistoric sequence can, in the manner of Cairnpapple in the early second millennium, be used as a key for the second half of the first millennium and the first three centuries of the Christian era. Another Shetland site, that on the island in a loch at *Clickhimin*, confirms and amplifies the Jarlshof sequence at certain points, and recent excavations in Tiree and elsewhere in the west have produced concordant results.

The first phase, which may be called *Jarlshof I*, consists of no recognisable structures but of deeply stratified layers of midden deposit with domestic debris alternating with sterile sand-blows. It is difficult to date this material, among which no metal occurs, but it is earlier than the second phase, of the seventh-sixth century B.C., and it may even be as old as the end of the second millennium B.C., but more likely to be within the first. *Jarlshof II* is a small group of stone-built houses which recognisably continue the architectural traditions of the Stanydale and other Shetland house-sites of the early or middle second millennium, and in its later phase was connected with a bronze-smith's workshop containing fragments of broken clay moulds for casting swords, socketed axe-heads, and pins of bronze. These are of a period of the later Scottish bronze industries known as the Adabrock phase, from a find in Lewis with an imported Continental bronze vessel of the seventh century B.C.: the phase runs from *c.* 650 B.C. for a century or two. At the other Shetland site mentioned, *Clickhimin I*, with a house of Jarlshof II type, is presumably contemporary.

The settlement of *Jarlshof III* which follows this shows a change in house-plans, now either simply circular, of the Jarlshof II type adapted to a circular plan; *Clickhimin II* again has a round house. This is the first appearance on these sites of the house of circular plan, characteristic of Scottish iron-using cultures until Early Christian times, as in England. In the British Isles the type goes back to the second and even the third millennium B.C., but it also seems to have been the type used by the Celtic peoples in Gaul and Iberia. In Jarlshof III there was a new type of pottery, comparable with that of the more southerly British earliest iron-using peoples, and indeed there was also slag from iron-working, showing a knowledge of the metal on the site. From now on, we are in an iron-using technology, utilising local resources, widely scattered and more abundant than the copper and tin previously needed for edge-tools. The Jarlshof III settlement does not necessarily follow immediately on Phase II, but it could date from any time from the fifth or fourth century B.C., the date of the earliest iron-using cultures in for instance Yorkshire.

At Clickhimin further building periods now follow. *Clickhimin III* is a phase marked by the building of a small stone-walled fort enclosing the island site, of two phases of construction, and *Clickhimin IV* is an extraordinary stone built "Blockhouse" structure set inside the fort entrance: these phases have been assigned to the late third and the first century B.C. respectively. The "Blockhouse" structure has a parallel in the fortification built across the neck of a promontory at the *Ness of Burgi* in Shetland. At Jarlshof the sequence is taken up again in *Jarlshof IV*, where a broch or circular defensive tower-house with a courtyard was built, probably in the first century A.D., and a similar broch on the Clickhimin site forms the *Clickhimin V* phase, of equivalent date. *Jarlshof V*, superseding the broch, was a circular house with stone piers to carry the roofing instead of timber uprights, and may be early second century A.D., and in the final prehistoric phase of *Jarlshof VI*, and in *Clickhimin VI* also, a development of this house-type with radial piers bounded back into the wall, the "wheelhouse", appears, probably in the early third century A.D.

With this key sequence in mind we may turn to the remaining monuments in chronological order. Among the most remarkable fortified sites in Scotland are those in which a massive stone wall has been reinforced by internal timbering, both horizontal and on occasion vertical as well. Such timber lacing can of course only be detected by excavation, and it provided an unfortunate hazard in an incendiary attack, when exposed beam-ends in the outer face caught fire, and this carried through the wall structure: the heat generated would be considerable and a wall built of stone with a low melting point could slump into irregular fused masses as it collapsed, producing the phenomena of the "vitrified forts", in which this condition can be seen on the surface. We thus know of a great many forts which originally had timber-laced walls, in addition to the unburnt examples recovered by excavation. This timber-lacing has a Continental history extending back to the ninth century B.C. at least, and was widely used in the early Celtic world. The only fort in the Ministry's charge which probably has a timber framework (it is not vitrified) is the massive inner stone structure on *The White Caterthun* in Angus, an elongated oval fort with huge double walls. Excavated forts of this type have produced occupation debris which could be as early as the third or second centuries B.C., but recent radiocarbon determinations appear to show that such constructions may go back to the fifth century, though as on the Continent the technique of timber-framing a fort wall may well have continued for centuries, and not all need be of the same date.

East Scotland since the middle eighth century B.C. had been in contact with the North German region to a degree unshared by Britain further south, and the Scottish timber-laced (and so the vitrified) forts might be derived from this region, where such fortification techniques were of long standing. In the context of these connections across the North Sea, extending for some centuries, we might find an archaeological situation in which the P-Celtic element in the Pictish language could have been transmitted.

Another type of enclosure, rather than fortification, is that of a palisade of timber uprights set in a bedding-trench cut in the subsoil. At *Castle Law Glencorse* (Midlothian) excavation has shown four periods of construction or occupation, of which the first phase, *Castle Law I*, is such a palisade, around which while it was still standing a defensive wall of stones and clay, *Castle Law II*, was later built, with horizontal timbering near its entrance gateway: a similar sequence has been found at Braidwood Fort nearby. Such palisade enclosures are widely distributed in southern Scotland and Northumberland, where one has a C_{14} date of *c.* 500 B.C., and another in Yorkshire is broadly contemporary, so that Castle Law I could date from the fourth or third century, but of course could also be later.

The "wall fort" of Castle Law II is comparable with many in southern Scotland, some overlying palisade enclosures, and in general earlier than defences formed by ramparts and ditches. A date from the third into the first century B.C. would be reasonable for such defences on the grounds of the archaeological material found associated with them on excavated sites; the inner wall fortification of *The Brown Caterthun* in Angus might belong here. *Castle Law III* is a refortification of the site by ramparts and rock-cut ditches, which could date from early in the first century B.C. or into the first A.D., and in this rather vague period might also come the multiple bank-and-ditch defences added to The Brown Caterthun, and those within which stands the broch at *Edinshall*, Berwickshire. The remarkable small but very heavily defended fort of *The Chesters*, Drem, East Lothian, where the inner of the multiple ramparts is overlain by circular stone-built huts, is likely, on analogy, to date from before the period of the Roman occupation of southern Scotland, when the *pax romana* rendered hill-forts obsolete and redundant. The secondary earthworks on The White Caterthun appear to be unfinished, and in common with several similar sites in eastern Scotland may represent abortive attempts at hurried defence against Roman forces. All these hill-forts represent an extension of the defensive traditions of southern England of the first three or four centuries B.C. The Scottish forts are much smaller than their contemporary English counterparts, and presumably relate to a Celtic society fragmented into smaller units than those in the south.

We have already touched on the brochs when outlining the Jarlshof and Clickhimin structural sequences. Examples in the Ministry's care (out of the 300 or so examples surviving from a probable total of about 500) comprise in Shetland not only the two just mentioned, but the most famous and tallest of all brochs, that of *Mousa*. In Orkney there are the brochs of *Gurness* on Mainland and *Midhowe* on Rousay; *Dun Carloway* in Lewis; in Inverness-shire the brochs of *Dun Telve* and *Dun Troddan* in Glenelg, and in Berwickshire the aberrant outlier within the fort at Edinshall already referred to.

The origin, function, cultural affinities, internal arrangements and roofing of brochs have for long been under discussion, and the debate continues, complicated partly by the paucity of adequately excavated examples, and partly by a tendency to generalise too widely from individual sites. While they have many features in common and are recognisably the product of a similar cultural background, brochs are numerous and very widely distributed in the west and north of Scotland, and built and occupied over a long period of time, with a resultant series of variations in detail, in a manner comparable to the chambered tombs discussed earlier. Structurally they are circular stone-built forts of a scale suitable to no more than a familial unit, with an average internal diameter of no more than 30 feet or so, with walls up to half that thickness with a single entrance, usually with lateral "guard-cells" in the wall thickness. Other cells may open from the inner court into the walls, which are ingeniously constructed as a double shell with spaces, galleries and stairs between, the two sides being tied together with transverse bonding slabs. This construction, generally carried up from ground level in the west and from a solid stone-built base in the northern group, allowed walls to be carried up to remarkable heights: Mousa, the highest surviving broch, still stands to a height of over 40 feet and may have been at least ten feet higher originally; Dun Troddan, Dun Telve and Dun Carloway stand to 30 feet and could have lost a proportionate amount of height. While we need not generalise too specifically from such examples, we are certainly dealing with defensive structures in which a height of 30 feet or more was probably not exceptional. In the brochs, one or two central hearths are normal, as in an ordinary circular house of the period in stone or timber, and various forms of roofing have been inferred, including a circular internal timber building range looking onto an open court with the hearth, as found within the fort wall of the third phase of Clickhimin.

The typological origin of the broch is clear: it is a strengthened and heightened version of a circular stone built house having in Scotland general prototypes in for instance those of Jarlshof III and Clickhimin II. These we saw could go back to the fourth or fifth century B.C., but on present showing we cannot carry brochs themselves back so far. The prototype for the circular house-plan behind the broch tradition, and that of the wheel-houses shortly to be described, is to be found among the Celtic iron-using peoples of southern England, as is the source for many other elements in the material culture of their builders, such as pottery, bone and metal types. All go together to indicate that we are seeing new intrusive groups of people colonising the Atlantic province of Scotland, with a southern ancestry and translating their timber-built circular houses into massive stone structures where wood was scanty or unobtainable, and defence at the family level at a premium.

The material culture of the broch builders indicates a date hardly before the first century B.C. for the earliest, and it seems that by the end of the first century A.D. the building of brochs died out, though in many instances they continued to be used as dwellings for several centuries to come. It is as if they had been produced as a type of defence in response to some situation, political or other, which had by the first century A.D. ceased to threaten. The scattered brochs in southern Scotland, such as Edinshall, must be late, perhaps in the early second century A.D., before the Severan campaigns from 209 rendered native fortifications impossible in the area. Some broch sites, for instance Midhowe and Gurness, have structures and fortifications outside their walls. The small hut-settlements appear to be secondary at both sites, and the massive defensive "forework" at the former may be contemporary with the broch or, as has been suggested, an earlier feature comparable and more or less contemporary with the blockhouse of Clickhimin IV, and the Ness of Burgi. At Gurness, the broch stands within the remains of a defensive fort wall and impressive double rock-cut ditches and ramparts, inturning to an entrance opposite that of the broch. These have been considered contemporary, but here and at Midhowe the excavation was not of the standard necessary to construct a reliable sequence of building and occupation.

Within the circular house tradition again come the wheelhouses found to be secondary to the broch in Jarlshof V and VI, and in Clickhimin VI. They represent a type widely distributed in the Atlantic province to the north and west, and on present showing do not date before the first century A.D. Their construction however, with free-standing or radial piers of stone supporting the roofing rafters, presupposes timber houses in which the function of the piers was fulfilled by upright posts of adequate scantling set in a ring between wall and central hearth. Such houses, as we saw, are widely known among British iron-working Celtic communities of the last three or four centuries B.C., and in Scotland, a Peeblesshire site with such a house could be dated by its pottery as early as the fifth century; the wheelhouse culture as a whole however has a southern ancestry.

We are left with a group of monuments representing the native iron-using cultures of Scotland during the later Roman occupation, as they seem in the main to belong to the second century A.D. These are the earth-houses or souterrains, the cellars of surface settlements now in most cases destroyed, as a subterranean structure has a far better survival value in the intensive agricultural areas in which so many souterrains occur. There is a considerable concentration of souterrains in the area to be that of the historical Pictish kingdom, and at *Ardestie* in Angus circular stone-built houses of such a farmstead survive; here and at the neighbouring site of *Carlungie*, and again at *Tealing* in Angus, and *Culsh*, Tarland, Aberdeenshire, the souterrain takes the normal form of an elongated trench dug in the subsoil, lined and roofed with slabs and stone walling, and with an entrance descending at one end. The site at *Grainbank*, Kirkwall, Orkney, is an outlier with a variant plan, and the souterrain constituting the phase of *Castle Law IV* is remarkable in having been dug into the silted-up hill-fort ditch of Castle Law III. Such souterrains are widely distributed in prehistoric and early historic contexts—Ireland, Cornwall, Brittany and West Jutland are among their areas of occurrence, and in Scotland the finds of such objects as Roman brooches and ornaments of the second century A.D., or the presence of re-used Roman carved stones in some south of the Forth, indicate their approximate date.

The later brochs, wheelhouses and souterrains are all prehistory side-by-side with history, which began in Scotland with the Agricolan campaigns of A.D. 80. As stone-using peoples overlapped with those using bronze, and these with the first iron-workers, and as early Celt and Pict lived adjacent to other tribes who spoke lost innominate tongues, so the later Celts and Picts continued their ancient way of life in areas unaffected by Roman rule, or where it saw no need to interfere with the archaic barbarian pattern of existence. The monuments representing the Romans in Scotland are of another order than those of prehistory, and form another, and very different, chapter.

THE ROMAN OCCUPATION

The Romans have left important monuments in Scotland. As might be expected in this wild frontier region, these are purely military in character. They may be classified under four heads: roads; marching camps; forts; and the frontier works on the Forth–Clyde isthmus. Many Roman forts have been identified in Scotland, and a number have been more or less explored. Of these latter, the most famous are Birrens on the Solway, the Roman *Blatobulgium*, and Newstead, *Trimontium*, on the Tweed. The excavation of Newstead, by the late Dr. James Curle in 1905–10, formed a landmark in the history of classical archaeology in western Europe. The northmost permanent fort so far known is at Cardean near Meigle in Angus. Thence a line of marching camps extends northwards at least as far as the Spey.

The most important Roman work remaining in Scotland is the Antonine Wall. The frontier line betwixt Forth and Clyde was first marked out by Julius Agricola in the year A.D. 80. Some of his small entrenched posts have been identified. In A.D. 142 or 143 the legate Lollius Urbicus, acting for the Emperor Antoninus Pius, laid out a permanent frontier on the Agricolan line. This consisted of a wall made of sods on a stone foundation, except in the eastern section, where the wall is of clay. In front was a ditch, deep and wide, and in the rear a military way. The garrison was disposed in some thirteen or more forts. The whole barrier is 37 miles long. It was held, but with at least two interruptions, till about the end of the second century. One of the Antonine Wall forts, *Rough Castle*, near Bonnybridge, Stirlingshire and three outstanding lengths of the Wall in Stirlingshire are in the custody of the Ministry.

THE MIDDLE AGES

THE ANGLO-NORMAN INFILTRATION

In Scotland it is usual to speak of the centuries between the Roman invasions and the Canmore dynasty as the early or Celtic period, and to restrict the terms Middle Ages, or medieval, to the period between the eleventh century and the Reformation. The distinction is a real one; for it was under the kings of the house of Canmore that Scotland was integrated into the medieval states-system as a strongly organized feudal monarchy, fashioned upon Anglo-Norman lines. In Scotland there was no Norman conquest in the English sense. We should speak rather of a Norman penetration. Under the generous patronage of the Canmore kings, from David I onwards, large numbers of Anglo-Norman settlers migrated into Galloway, Lothian, the Central Lowlands and the north-eastern plains. Sometimes by Crown grants, at other times by marrying Celtic heiresses, they obtained extensive estates. Everywhere they introduced the feudal system, and its outward and visible symbol, the feudal castle—the private stronghold of a territorial magnate exercising devolved administrative and judical authority over his tenantry. These castles were not the ponderous stone keeps of popular imagination. Even in England such costly structures were exceptional. The ordinary Norman castle was a thing not of stone and lime but of timbered earthwork—a moated mound crowned by a palisade enclosing a wooden tower. Often there was also a banked and palisaded courtyard sheltering the household buildings, likewise in wood. We may see pictures of these structures on the Bayeux Tapestry; and they were almost the only kind of castle that existed in Scotland during the Norman penetration in the twelfth century. The Norman name for them is a *motte;* where a courtyard is attached, it is known as the *bailey*, and the entire construction may be described as a *motte* and *bailey*, or a mount and bailey castle. One of the finest in Scotland, *Duffus Castle*, near Elgin, is now in the Ministry's care. It has been crowned by later stone buildings which have slipped down the Norman earthworks.

Parallel to the introduction of the Anglo-Norman baronage with their earthwork castles came the Anglo-Norman clergy bringing the Roman discipline and organization, as they had developed on the soil of the old Empire during the centuries when Celtic Scotland was largely isolated from the European states-system. Gradually the country was divided up into parishes, each served by a parochial priest, and the parishes were grouped into dioceses, each presided over by a bishop. So alongside the feudal castle two new items, the parish church and the cathedral, were added to the Scottish scene. In many cases the parish was just the manor of a feudal baron, ecclesiastically considered, and the parish church began as the private chapel of the lord of the manor. That is why to this day in Scotland the remains of a Norman castle are so often found close beside the parish church. Church and castle, side by side, represent respectively the ecclesiastical and the civil nuclei of the early parochial organisation.

The parish priests, with their bishops, deans and other dignified superiors, were known as the secular clergy. Alongside them were introduced the regular or monastic clergy—the Benedictine and Cistercian monks, and the Augustinian canons who were a kind of intermediate clergy, living the cloistered life of monks, yet capable of undertaking a cure of souls like the parish priests. The kings of the Canmore dynasty, led by David I, were notable founders of monasteries, partly in response to the religious impulse of the time, and partly because the abbeys were civilizing agents in a wild, untutored countryside.

By the close of the thirteenth century, as a result of all these complex processes, the infeudation of at least the Scottish Lowlands had been completed. Anglo-Norman civilization was everywhere predominant, and the four chief elements in the medieval landscape—the feudal castles, the parochial churches, the cathedrals, and the abbeys—were conspicuous wherever the Norman penetration had reached. Also to the same great formative period belongs the foundation of the burghs, centres of trade and industry, established by kings, barons, or prelates, and colonized by Anglo-Norman or Flemish craftsmen and merchants. Scotland was now, comparatively speaking, a strongly organized feudal monarchy, able to resist the onslaught of Plantagenet imperialism seeking to complete the Norman conquest by force of arms, where already much of its work had been accomplished by peaceful infiltration.

CASTLES. Of the four chief elements in the medieval scene, the castles first may claim our attention. During the thirteenth century—the "Golden Age" of Alexander II and III—the earliest stone castles made their appearance in Scotland. Perhaps the oldest of these, in a typological sense, is *Castle Sween*, in Knapdale; with its great rectangular buttresses it recalls Norman construction. The finer castles of this prosperous era, such as *Dirleton*, *Hailes*, *Caerlaverock*, *Kildrummy* and *Bothwell*, are beautifully built of dressed ashlar, and have large round towers flanking curtain walls which enclose a courtyard. In these castles we may still see the destruction caused by the Scots during the struggle for independence, in accordance with Bruce's well-known policy, which was to dismantle such strongholds on their recapture from the English.

In the fourteenth century great rectangular tower-houses make their appearance, like *Threave* or *Loch Leven*. Later still these tower-houses came to be built with a wing—or "jamb", to use the Scottish term— added on one side, giving a plan like the letter L. Good examples are *Affleck Castle*, near Dundee, *Scotstarvit Tower* in Fife, and *Auchindoun* in Glenfiddich. This plan of a tower-house, whether on the simple rect-angular or on the L-design, remained a favourite one among the smaller lairds until the end of the castle-building period. A late instance of its persistence is *Greenknowe Tower*, Berwickshire.

In the fourteenth and fifteenth centuries some larger castles continued to be built on the old plan of long and high curtain walls with round flanking towers. Two impressive examples are *Caerlaverock* and *Tantallon*. At both we can see how elaborately designed suites or lodgings came to be erected within the enclosure. Gradually it became the custom to group these symmetrically round the courtyard, and the tendency is to mass the principal apartments frontally. This process may be studied, in various forms, at the large castles of *Crichton*, *Craigmillar*, *Huntly* and *Balvenie*, and at *Linlithgow Palace*.

The introduction of firearms, and particularly of hand-guns such as could be used in the defence of a laird's house, led to the evolution of a type of castle consisting of a central mass with wings or towers echeloned at diagonally opposite corners, like the letter Z. Each tower flanks two sides of the main building, which in turn commands the towers, so that the defensive arrangement is complete. The wings or towers also supplied much additional accommodation; and, holding on as it were by their finger-tips to the central structure, they interfered as little as possible with its lighting. Excellent examples of this intriguing design are *Glenbuchat* in Strathdon, and *Claypotts* at Dundee. At *Tolquhon* we see the device adapted to a courtyard castle. Perhaps the most impressive example of the Z-plan, however, is to be found at *Noltland Castle* in the remote island of Westray, in Orkney. With its tiers of yawning gun-loops, it resembles an old man-o'-war's hulk.

Scottish castellated architecture reaches its climax about the turn of the sixteenth and seventeenth centuries. Much of the landed property of the ancient church had fallen into the hands of the lairds, and their new-found wealth expressed itself in an outburst of building. More settled internal conditions, and the end of wars with England after the Union of the Crowns, were also circumstances favourable to architecture. To this period, accordingly, we owe such splendid pieces of early Renaissance work as Nithsdale's building at Caerlaverock, the remarkable diamonded façade at Crichton, and the upper part of Huntly Castle with its stately row of oriels. The most original design of this period is the garden wall at *Edzell Castle*, with its profuse heraldic display and its series of sculptured panels of the Planetary Deities, the Liberal Arts and the Cardinal Virtues.

CATHEDRALS. Of Scottish Cathedrals, *Glasgow*, *St. Andrews*, *Dunkeld*, *Dunblane*, *Fortrose*, *Aberdeen* (the transepts only) and *Elgin*, are in the Ministry's care. The Cathedral Church of Glasgow is still complete, with the exception of two western towers, unhappily taken down in the last century. The main mass of the building is a splendid essay in the high noontide of the Gothic style, as it had developed in Britain about the year 1300. There is nothing specially Scottish about it, either in plan or in detail, since it was ordained, and mostly completed, before the War of Independence had severed Scotland's friendly relations with her southern neighbour and embarked her upon a course of intense, self-centred nationalism which would lead to the growth of a national style in her architecture. The design of the Cathedral is unique in Scotland, because it is all set out upon the central theme of St. Mungo's shrine, housed in a beautiful crypt under the presbytery. It has a broad, square-ended ambulatory round the shrine, within which the eastern end of the presbytery, likewise square, rises with a most imposing effect. According to the usual Scottish practice, the aisles are vaulted, while the nave and choir retain their fine medieval timber roofs.

The Cathedrals of St. Andrews and Elgin likewise belong in the main to the period before the War of Independence. Of St. Andrews Cathedral little save the ground plan, with the east gable, half of the west gable, and portions of the south transept have escaped destruction. About 390 feet in length, as originally designed, with a nave of fourteen bays, this was the longest church in Scotland. Beside the great Gothic cathedral stands its tiny Romanesque predecessor, the *Church of St. Rule*, or *St. Regulus*, built between 1126 and 1144. It consists of a choir, a sanctuary, and a tall square tower, west of which a nave was subsequently added. St. Rule's was built by Yorkshire masons, but the great height of its tower seems to betray Celtic influence.

The Cathedral Church of St. Mary, at Elgin, is likewise now a sorry ruin, though much more of it remains than at St. Andrews. It is unique in possessing double aisles, and the effect produced by its interior must have been one of vast spaciousness, rather than the long perspective at which medieval builders usually aimed in Britain. Strong French feeling pervades the earlier work of the church. In 1390 it was burned by the Wolf of Badenoch, being described on that melancholy occasion as "the pride of the land, the glory of the realm, the delight of wayfarers and strangers, a praise and a boast among foreign nations." To the restoration carried out in the fifteenth century belong some of the loveliest portions of the fabric, notably the vaulting of the octagonal chapter house.

The choir and presbytery of Dunkeld Cathedral have been restored and are in use as the parish church. This part of the structure retains some traces of early thirteenth century work; but the nave and west tower are a most interesting specimen of the vigorous style of two centuries later, when Scottish church architecture had taken on a strongly national cast. The plain cylindrical drums of the nave arcade, resembling those of Aberdeen Cathedral, represent a harking back to Romanesque fashion which is one of the marks of the later Scottish style. In the sanctuary is the tomb of the Wolf of Badenoch, who, notwithstanding his destruction of Elgin Cathedral, died at peace with Holy Church, and, royal ruffian as he was, was buried as beseemed a prince of the blood. The situation of Dunkeld Cathedral, on a lovely reach of the Tay, and backed by dark wooded and rocky hills, is one of great beauty. Its most famous Bishop was the poet, Gavin Douglas, the fifteenth century translator of the Aeneid, who

> "in a barbarous age,
> Gave to rude Scotland Virgil's page."

PAROCHIAL AND COLLEGIATE CHURCHES. Of simple parish churches dating from the Middle Ages the Ministry of Public Building and Works now has a number under its care up and down the country. Among these may be mentioned the churches of *Kinkell, Auchindoir* and *Deskford*, in the north-east, with their remarkable sacrament houses, witnesses to an artistic impulse generated by the good Bishops Elphinstone and Dunbar, and their cultured factor, Alexander Galloway, rector of Kinkell; *St. Bride's Church*, Douglas, with its fine monuments of that famous fighting race; and a remarkable group of early churches in the Orkney Islands, including the unique round church at *Orphir*—a twelfth century structure, whose remoter prototype must be sought in the Church of the Holy Sepulchre at Jerusalem. To the same period belongs the church at *Egilsay*, with a round tower built in its western gable. It is dedicated to St. Magnus, and stands on or near the site of his martyrdom.

In a class by itself stands the early sixteenth century *Church of St. Clement* at Rodel in the Isle of Harris. Cruciform in plan, with a conspicuous western tower, it is the only church of a monumental character in the outer isles. Its ornate architectural detail recalls that of Iona, and exhibits the same Irish influence and persistence of "retarded" motives. This church contains the elaborate tomb of Alastair Crottach—"the hump-backed"— eighth chief of the MacLeods of Harris and Dunvegan.

In the later Middle Ages the foundation of collegiate churches took the place of the great monasteries which had provided an outlet for the piety of an earlier generation. Such an establishment of collegiate priests was usually planted by the noble founder in the immediate neighbourhood of his residence, and a chief item in the duties of the corporation would be to celebrate mass daily for the souls of the founder and his kin. The Ministry now has five of these collegiate churches under its charge—*Maybole, Dunglass, Seton, Castle Semple* and *Lincluden*. The militarization of Scottish life, owing to the chronic war with England, had a curious result in giving these later churches a half baronial appearance. They are furnished with the battlements, crow-stepped gables, heavy vaults, and pack-saddle roofs of the feudal stronghold. This castellar effect reaches its climax in the *Preceptory Church* of the Knights Hospitallers at *Torphichen*. The least martial, and the most beautiful, of these collegiate churches is Lincluden. Its choir is a virginal piece of purest Decorated Gothic, and the tomb of the Princess Margaret Stewart, daughter of Robert III, is, perhaps, the finest thing of its kind in Scotland. Here, too, we have a well-preserved range of collegiate buildings attached to the church—the nave of which, as often in such structures, was never built.

ABBEYS. Of all the monuments in the nation's custody none are more popular than the abbeys. The rare architectural beauty of the buildings themselves, the picturesque surroundings in which most of them are situated, and the historic events and personages or literary figures with which they are connected, have combined to fix them in the public affection. Scotland is fortunate in that her four famous Border monasteries —Kelso, Melrose, Jedburgh, and Dryburgh—are all in the national keeping. In some respects the mighty ruin of *Kelso*, towering above the little town "like some antique Titan predominating over the dwarfs of a later world," is the most interesting of them all. Almost wholly in the Romanesque style, its remains are of unique importance, because the design of the church has been of Carolingian type, with transepts and a tower at both ends, east and west. *Jedburgh Abbey* is likewise mainly a Romanesque building, and, like Kelso, has a special interest for the architectural antiquary. It shows a series of heavy arches spanning the bays of the choir, arcades below the triforium, the main piers being carried right up above the latter. This arrangement is obviously an imperfect recollection of the "underslung" triforium at Oxford Cathedral. To *Melrose* belongs the literary glamour cast around its ruins by Sir Walter Scott, while the Abbey Church itself, almost wholly rebuilt after its destruction by Richard II, in 1385, is a rare and precious example of Scottish Decorated work, though the influence of English Perpendicular tracery is strongly evident on the great east window. Loveliest of all the Border abbeys, in itself and in its setting is *Dryburgh*, hallowed by the graves of Scott and Haig.

The three Cistercian abbeys of Galloway—*Dundrennan, Glenluce*, and

Sweetheart or *New Abbey*—are likewise in the nation's custody. Dundrennan, a splendid ruin, saw the last that Scotland saw of the hapless Queen Mary; while the beautiful remains of Sweetheart Abbey are forever sanctified by the touching story of its origin as the abiding memorial of a great lady's love of her long dead lord. Though overshadowed by the royal palace which adjoins it, there is in all Scotland no choicer specimen of medieval church architecture than the nave of *Holyrood Abbey*. Although the building had been of no more than moderate size, its western front, with a rich portal between the towers, was one of the grandest things of its kind in Scotland. At *Arbroath Abbey* we have the imposing remains of another royal foundation, dedicated by William the Lion to the honour of St. Thomas of Canterbury. The impressive fortified gatehouse is an unusual feature, and the Abbot's House is the best example left in Scotland.

When the word "abbey" is mentioned, there naturally rises before our minds the vision of a great church. Yet it is the cloister (Latin, *claustrum*), not the church, which is the essential of the monastery; for a monk is a member of Society who by their vows are cloistered, *clausi*, or shut off from the world within the bounds of their cloister garth, or that, removed from the world's distractions, they may spend their time in prayer for the souls of the founders and benefactors of their house. It is, therefore the cloister and its buildings, rather than the church, that gives us the deepest insight into the life of a monastic community. Of the abbeys in the care of the Ministry of Public Building and Works, none illustrates these claustral buildings more completely than the lovely island monastery of *Inchcolm*, in the Firth of Forth. Doubtless it owes its preservation to its insular position.

THE ROYAL PALACES. In a category by themselves stand the two great national citadels of *Edinburgh* and *Stirling*, and the royal palaces of *Linlithgow* and *Holyroodhouse*. Round the castled rocks of Edinburgh and Stirling much of Scotland's turbulent history has been acted, and it is a consequence of their stormy record that the buildings in both cases are, for the most part, of comparatively modern date. At *Edinburgh* the oldest portion surviving is the little Romanesque chapel of St. Margaret. Inside the Half-moon Battery, constructed by the Regent Morton, there is still to be seen a considerable fragment of David's Tower, erected by David II between 1368 and 1379, and destroyed in the bombardment of 1573, after which the Battery was erected on top of its ruined stump. The Great Hall, with its hammer-beam roof, and the Royal Apartments are mostly of the sixteenth and seventeenth centuries. At *Stirling*, Cochrane's Hall, built by the unlucky favourite of James III, has been, perhaps, the finest thing of its kind in Scotland, while the Royal Apartments, erected by French masons, are an early and quaint example of Renaissance architecture. In James III's gatehouse and the batteries of Queen Anne's reign in front of it, we may study the difference between medieval ideas of fortification and those evolved after cannon had revolutionized the arts of attack and defence. The Chapel Royal was built by James VI for the christening of his son, Prince Henry, in 1594.

> *"Lithgow, whose palyce of plesance*
> *Micht be ane pattern in Portugall and France"*;

—so wrote Sir David Lindsay of the Mount in the reign of James V; and *Linlithgow Palace* deserved all his praise, for it is without doubt the finest piece of old domestic architecture left to us in Scotland. Although built at different periods from the early fifteenth century onwards, it displays a surprising uniformity in design. Its situation, overlooking the loch, remains in all its unspoiled beauty, and the great fifteenth century town's kirk, which closely adjoins it, combines with the Palace to form a group of medieval architecture unsurpassed in the country.

The *Palace of Holyroodhouse* is indelibly associated with the tragic history of Mary Stewart, and the rooms that figured in Rizzio's murder still survive in James IV's tower: but the rest of the palace was built between 1671 and 1699 by Sir William Bruce for Charles II. A modern critic has justly observed that it "possesses a sort of refined and cultured individuality which can hardly be claimed for the great contemporary palaces of the mainland, though one of them is renowned Versailles."

NOTES

The following list of monuments in Scotland in the care of the Ministry of Public Building and Works includes a brief description of each monument and information about access and admission. Map references are taken from the O.S. 1″ Map of Great Britain, 7th Series, and distances are given as the crow flies.

Guide Books are obtainable at monuments where shown. They may also be obtained from Her Majesty's Stationery Office—see cover. At a number of monuments for which guide books are not yet available, the custodian has a few handboards on which the history of the building is recorded.

Postcards and in some cases colour transparencies are on sale at monuments marked with an asterisk.

Photographs may not be taken at the Palace of Holyroodhouse but may be taken elsewhere without a permit except at buildings occupied by the Military where special permission may sometimes be necessary. The use of stand cameras is subject to the discretion of the custodian.

Admission Fees. These are indicated under each monument.

Children under fifteen years of age and Old-Age Pensioners on production of their pension books are admitted at half price. At monuments other than Edinburgh Castle and the Palace of Holyroodhouse parties of eleven visitors and upwards may claim a rebate of 10% on the admission charge paid for the party.

Season Tickets, price 15s. adult, 7s. 6d. child and Old-Age Pensioners on production of their pension books, valid for one year, admit the holder to any Monument in the Ministry's charge. They may be obtained from The Clerk of Stationery, Ministry of Public Building and Works, Argyle House, 3 Lady Lawson Street, Edinburgh EH3 9SD.

Standard Hours of Admission are:

	Weekdays	Sundays
April—September	9.30 a.m.—7 p.m.	2 p.m.—7 p.m.
October—March	10 a.m.—4.30 p.m.	2 p.m.—4.30 p.m.

Variations from the Standard Hours are noted under the particular monument.

ABERDEENSHIRE

Brandsbutt Stone

A fine Pictish symbol stone, with a well-preserved ogham inscription. The stone was broken up to build into a field dyke, but the pieces have now been put together. Originally it formed one of a circle.

Situation. At Brandsbutt Farm, about 1 mile N.W. of centre of Inverurie. On Route A 96. O.S. 1″ map sheet 40, ref. NJ 760224.

Admission. All times without charge.

Corgarff Castle

A sixteenth century tower house, converted into a garrison post and enclosed within a star-shaped loopholed wall in 1748. Traditionally built in 1537 as a hunting seat; the scene of the burning of Margaret Forbes and her family by the Gordons in 1571; featured in the campaigns of Montrose (1645) and in all the Jacobite risings; occupied by Hanoverian troops after 1746 as a base for maintaining order in the district.

Situation. ½ mile south-west of Cock Bridge on the Strathdon–Tomintoul road (A 939). O.S. 1" map sheet 38, ref. NJ 255086.

Admission. May be viewed from outside.

Cullerlie Stone Circle

A sepulchral stone circle of eight undressed boulders enclosing an area consecrated by fires on which eight small cairns were later constructed; probably of late second millennium date.

Situation. 1 mile south of Garlogie, 9 miles west of Aberdeen on Aberdeen–Echt road (A 974). O.S. 1" map sheet 40, ref. NJ 785043.

Admission. All times without charge.

Culsh Earth-House

A well preserved example of an earth-house with roofing slabs intact over large chamber and entrance; of Iron Age date.

Situation. At Culsh Farm, 2 miles north-east of Tarland. O.S. 1" map sheet 39, ref. NJ 505055.

Admission. All times without charge.

*Deer Abbey

The remains of a Cistercian monastery founded by William Comyn, Earl of Buchan, in 1219. Its predecessor, the Celtic Abbey associated with the famous *Book of Deer*, was on a different site. Of the abbey church little remains, but portions of the conventual buildings stand to a fair height, and the foundations of the whole have been revealed by excavations. The church dates from the thirteenth century, but the other buildings were much reconstructed in late medieval times. The abbey is beautifully situated within a walled precinct on the banks of the River South Ugie.

Situation. Near Old Deer, 10 miles west of Peterhead. O.S. 1" map sheet 31, ref. NJ 969481.

Hours of Admission. April–September—standard, but notice posted when keyholder absent. Closed in winter.

Admission Fee. 1s.

Official Guide Pamphlet. 6d.

Dyce Symbol Stones

In the ruined parish church are preserved two fine examples of Pictish symbol stones. One is of the older type, with incised symbols only, while in the other the symbols are accompanied by a Celtic cross, and the sculpture is in relief and decorated with Celtic patterns.

Situation. At Dyce Old Church, 2 miles north-west of Dyce, near Aberdeen. Approached from Dyce–Pitmedden road. O.S. 1" map sheet 40, ref. NJ 875154.

Admission. All times without charge.

East Aquhorthies Stone Circle

One of a group of stone circles of a type found mainly in this part of Scotland (*c.* 1800–1600 B.C.). The circle of upright stones is almost complete. The large recumbent slab is accompanied by two others which project into the circle. *Situation.* 2½ miles west of Inverurie. O.S. 1″ map sheet 40, ref. NJ 733208. *Admission.* All times without charge.

Glenbuchat Castle

An ancient seat of the Gordons, occupying a commanding position on upper Donside. It was built in 1590, and is a fine example of the Z-plan, having a square tower at each of two diagonally opposite corners. The stair turrets are supported, not on the usual corbelling, but by *trompes* or squinch arches in the French manner. Its last laird, John Gordon, played a notable part in the two Jacobite risings of 1715 and 1745. He escaped after Culloden and died in exile.

Situation. 14 miles west of Alford on Cambus o' May road (A 97). O.S. 1″ map sheet 39, ref. NJ 398149.

Admission. Not yet open to public. May be viewed from outside.

Official Guide Book for Kildrummy and Glenbuchat. 1s. 9d. On sale at Kildrummy.

*Huntly Castle

One of the noblest baronial ruins in Scotland, this castle was the headquarters of the "gay Gordons". In the 16th and 17th centuries its rulers, the Earls and Marquises of Huntly, were the most powerful magnates in the north, and leaders of the Catholic cause in the Counter-reformation struggle. The site is a Norman one, and is still marked by the earth-works of a large motte and bailey. On the east side is a ravelin perhaps dating from the Civil War. The remains of the stone castle comprise the foundations of a strong 15th century tower-house, destroyed in 1594, and an imposing hall-house or "palace", with a great round tower and a smaller one containing the stair. The heraldic enrichments of this building are the most elaborate in Scotland, and its row of oriels are a reminiscence of Blois. The castle stands in a beautifully timbered park beside the rocky gorge of the Deveron, here spanned by an ancient bridge.

Situation. ½ mile north of Huntly. O.S. 1″ map sheet 30, ref. NJ 532407.

Hours of Admission. Standard.

Admission Fee. 1s.

Official Guide Book. 1s. 9d.

*Kildrummy Castle

"The noblest of northern castles", and the most complete example in Scotland of a secular building dating from the 13th century. The wall of *enceinte*, with four round towers, in greater or lesser preservation, the hall, and the chapel with its fine three-light window, belong in substance to the original fabric. The great gatehouse is Edwardian, and there is later work of the 15th and 16th centuries. The barbican with its drawbridge pit is of considerable interest. This castle was the seat of the Earls of Mar, and played a memorable part in Scottish history from the Wars of Independence until the "Fifteen", when it was dismantled.

Situation. 10 miles west of Alford on Cambus o' May road (A 97). O.S. 1″ map sheet 39, ref. NJ 455164.
Admission. All times without charge.
Official Guide Book for Kildrummy and Glenbuchat. 1s. 9d.

Kinkell Church

The ruins of an early sixteenth century parish church, with some ornate details, including a rich sacrament house of unusual design, dated 1524. In the church is the monument of Gilbert de Greenlaw, slain at the battle of Harlaw (1411).
Situation. On the Don, 2 miles south-south-east of Inverurie. O.S. 1″ map sheet 40, ref. NJ 786191.
Admission. All times without charge.

Loanhead Stone Circle

The best known example of a widespread group of recumbent stone circles in east Scotland; the circle enclosed a kerbed ring cairn built over the site of a cremation pyre; dates to the period *c.* 1800–1600 B.C. but was in use at a later date.
Situation. ¼ mile north-west of hamlet of Daviot, 5 miles north-north-west of Inverurie. O.S. 1″ map sheet 40, ref. NJ 748288.
Admission. All times without charge.

Maiden Stone

The most famous of the Early Christian monuments in Aberdeenshire, this stone is associated with several weird legends formerly current in the Garioch. On one side it displays a richly ornamented Celtic cross and other decoration in the same style, and on the other side are Pictish symbols.
Situation. Near Chapel of Garioch, 4½ miles north-west of Inverurie (by Drumdurno Farm). O.S. 1″ map sheet 40, ref. NJ 703247.
Admission. All times without charge.

Memsie Burial Cairn

A fine example of a large stone-built cairn probably dating to *c.* 1500 B.C.
Situation. Near the village of Memsie, 3 miles south-south-west of Fraserburgh on route A 981. O.S 1″ map sheet 31, ref. NJ 977621.
Admission. All times without charge.

Peel Ring of Lumphanan

Major early medieval earthwork, consisting of a large oval motte or mound defended by a wet ditch. Masonry foundations can be traced on the summit. Lumphanan is said to have been the scene of Macbeth's final defeat in 1057, and was visited by Edward I of England in 1296.
Situation. ½ mile south-west of Lumphanan and 22 miles west of Aberdeen (route A. 980). O.S. 1″ map sheet 39, ref. NJ 577037.
Admission. All times without charge.

Picardy Stone

A Pictish symbol stone of the oldest class, with incised symbols.
Situation. Near Myreton, 2 miles north-west of Insch (route A 979). O.S. 1"
map sheet 39, ref. NJ 610303.
Admission. All times without charge.

St. Machar's Cathedral, Aberdeen

Only the nave, western towers, and transepts of this cathedral now remain.
The nave is in use as a parish church, but the transepts are ruined and under
the guardianship of the Ministry. The two west piers of the crossing date
from *c.* 1380 and show figure sculpture and "knife-cut" foliage, closely
resembling contemporary work at Melrose. In the south transept is the fine
altar tomb of Bishop Dunbar (1514–32).
Situation. In Old Aberdeen, 1½ miles north of city centre. O.S. 1" map sheet
40, ref. NJ 939088.
Admission. All times without charge.

St. Mary's Church, Auchindoir

One of the finest medieval parish churches remaining in Scotland; roofless but
otherwise entire. It has a rich Norman–Transitional doorway, some good
First Pointed details, and a beautiful early sixteenth century sacrament house
(*cf.* Deskford, Kinkell). There are also some interesting sixteenth century
heraldic monuments.
Situation. On by-road (B 9002) ½ mile west of main Aberdeen–Huntly road
(A 944) between Lumsden and Rhynie. O.S. 1" map sheet 39, ref. NJ 477246.
Admission. All times without charge.

Tarves Medieval Tomb

A fine altar-tomb of William Forbes, the laird who enlarged Tolquhon Castle.
It shows an interesting commixture of Gothic and Renaissance styles.
Situation. In the kirkyard of Tarves, 15 miles north-north-west of Aberdeen
and 4 miles north-east of Oldmeldrum. O.S. 1" map sheet 40, ref. NJ 869312.
Admission. All times without charge.

★Tolquhon Castle

A seat of the Forbes family. Its nucleus is a strong rectangular tower, dating
from the early fifteenth century. To this was added, between 1584 and 1589,
a large quadrangular mansion, now roofless, but otherwise in a very complete
state of preservation. This mansion admirably illustrates the great advance
in domestic planning during the reign of James VI. A notable feature is the
gatehouse with its two round towers, armorial bearings, and quaint figure
sculpture. The castle is remarkable for the variety of its ornate gun-loops.
There is a large forecourt with outbuildings, and a spacious pleasance, still
graced by rows of venerable yews and hollies.
Situation. 15 miles north-north-east of Aberdeen off the Pitmedden–Tarves
road (B 999). O.S. 1" map sheet 40, ref. NJ 874286.
Hours of Admission. Standard.
Admission Fee. 1s.
Official Guide Pamphlet. 6d.

Tomnaverie Stone Circle

The remains of a recumbent stone circle probably *c.* 1800–1600 B.C. Unexcavated.

Situation. Near Mill of Wester Coull, about 4 miles north-west of Aboyne and 1 mile south-east of Tarland (B 9094). O.S. 1″ map sheet 39, ref. NJ 488035.

Admission. All times without charge.

ANGUS

Aberlemno Sculptured Stones

Consisting of a splendid upright cross-slab, with Pictish symbols and figure sculpture on the reverse, in Aberlemno kirkyard, and three stones beside the road (B 9134), one of which bears incised symbols and another a cross and dragonesque creatures in front, and symbols and figure sculpture on the reverse.

Situation. At Aberlemno, 5 miles north-east of Forfar. O.S. 1″ map sheet 50, ref. NO 523555 and 523559.

Admission. All times without charge.

*Affleck Castle

A late fifteenth century tower-house on the L-plan, still in perfect condition. Four storeys in height, turretted and battlemented, it is noteworthy for the elaborate and advanced character of its internal arrangements. Off the solar, or upper hall, there is a very beautiful little chapel, or oratory, and the solar itself is a room of exceptional distinction, which, despite its small size, has few equals in Scotland. The castle was the residence of the ancient family of Auchinleck or Affleck of that ilk.

Situation. At Monikie, 8 miles north-east of Dundee. O.S. 1″ map sheet 50, ref. NO 495388.

Admission. All reasonable times, except Sundays, on application to custodian, but notice posted when he is absent.

Admission Fee. 1s.

Official Guide Pamphlet. 3d.

*Arbroath Abbey

The imposing remains of a Tironensian monastery founded in 1176 by William the Lion. It was dedicated to St. Thomas of Canterbury. Here in 1320 a great assembly of the nation issued the famous Declaration of Arbroath, in which, they asserted Scottish independence against the encroachments of Plantagenet England. Considerable portions of the cruciform abbey church remain, including an aisleless presbytery, transeptal chapels and two western towers. The best preserved portion is the south transept, with its rose window. The great west doorway had above it a tribune, like those at Holyrood and St. Andrews. Important remains of the claustral buildings also survive, including the "pend" or vaulted entrance, the embattled "regality tower" and the abbot's house, which has been restored as a museum.

Situation. In Arbroath. O.S. 1″ map sheet 50, ref. NO 644414.

Hours of Admission. Standard.

Admission Fee. 1s.

Official Guide Book. 2s. 3d. The Guide Book to Early Christian and Pictish Monuments of Scotland is also available. Price 5s.

D

Ardestie and Carlungie Earth-houses

Two examples of large earth-houses attached to surface dwellings. At Ardestie the gallery is curved and 80 feet in length; the Carlungie souterrain is 150 feet long and is most complex; used in first centuries A.D.

Situation. About 7 miles east of Dundee north of route A 92. O.S. 1″ map sheet 50, ref. NO 502344 and 511359.

Admission. All times without charge.

Brechin: Maison Dieu Chapel

This is an interesting fragment of mid-thirteenth century ecclesiastical architecture. The ruins consist of a portion of the south wall of the chapel and a small extent of the east wall. The details of the doors and windows are unusually fine. The chapel is said to have been founded in 1256 by William de Brechin. The structure, as the name implies, doubtless formed part of a hospital.

Situation. In the centre of the town of Brechin. O.S. 1″ map sheet 50, ref. NO 598604.

Admission. All reasonable times, on application to custodian.

Brechin: Round Tower

One of the two remaining round towers of the Irish type in Scotland (see also ABERNETHY, PERTHSHIRE). It dates from about 1000 and is now attached to the thirteenth century cathedral. The doorway with its figure sculpture is of a characteristic Irish design. The spire is an addition of the fourteenth century.

Situation. In Brechin. O.S. 1″ map sheet 50, ref. NO 596601.

Admission. Can be viewed from the churchyard.

Broughty Castle

A large oblong structure with a battlemented top; erected about the beginning of the sixteenth century.

Situation. In Broughty Ferry. O.S. 1″ map sheet 50, ref. NO 465304.

Admission. Administered by Dundee Corporation. There is an associated museum illustrating the history of the Castle and Broughty Ferry, whaling, the natural history of the Tay, arms and armour and furniture.

Weekdays, except Fridays, 11 a.m.–1 p.m. and 2 p.m.–5 p.m.

Sundays, 2 p.m.–5 p.m.

For School and other party visits write (or phone) The Assistant in Charge, Broughty Castle Museum, Broughty Ferry, Dundee DD5 2BE. (Tel. 0826 76121)

The Caterthuns:

The Brown Caterthun

An excellent example of Iron Age hill fort with four concentric ramparts and ditches interrupted by entrances and causeways. Unexcavated.

The White Caterthun

A well-preserved hill fort of the Iron age with massive stone rampart and defensive ditch and outer earthworks.

Situation. Near the village of Menmuir, about 5 miles north-west of Brechin. O.S. 1″ map sheet 50, ref. NO 555668 and 548660.

Admission. All times without charge.

*Claypotts (Plate 22)

This tower house bears the dates 1569 and 1588, and was a seat of the Strachan family. Later it belonged to the celebrated John Graham of Claverhouse, Viscount Dundee. It is still roofed and is a fine example of a fortified residence on the "three-stepped" or Z-plan, having a round tower at each of two diagonally opposite corners. These towers are corbelled out to form overhanging cap-houses in a remarkably picturesque manner. The ground floor of the castle is well provided with wide-mouthed gun-loops.

Situation. 3½ miles east of Dundee at junction between A 92 and B 978. O.S. 1″ map sheet 50, ref. NO 453318.

Hours of Admission. Standard.

Admission Fee. 1s.

Official Guide Book. 1s.

Eassie Sculptured Stone

A fine example of the elaborately sculptured Early Christian monuments of Angus. On the front is a richly decorated Celtic cross, with figure and animal subjects, and on the back are Pictish symbols and processional scenes.

Situation. In the old churchyard of Eassie off the Glamis–Meigle road (A 94). O.S. 1″ map sheet 50, ref. NO 353475.

Admission. All times without charge.

*Edzell Castle (Plate 23)

This, the home of the Lindsays of Glenesk, was the finest castle in Angus. The oldest part is a tower-house, dating from the early sixteenth century. To this a quadrangular mansion was added later in that century; and in 1602 the buildings were completed with a spacious walled garden or pleasance, a bath-house and summer-house. The garden wall exhibits a display of heraldic and symbolical decoration unique in Britain, including a series of sculptured panels portraying the Cardinal Virtues, the Liberal Arts, and the Planetary Deities. These subjects have been shown to be of German inspiration.

Situation. 1 mile west of Edzell, 5 miles north of Brechin. O.S. 1″ map sheet 50, ref. NO 585691.

Hours of Admission. Standard.

Admission Fee. 1s.

Official Guide Book. 1s.

Restenneth Priory

A house of Augustinian canons regular, probably founded by David I. It was burned by Edward I, but recovered its prosperity under the patronage of Robert Bruce, a son of whom, Prince Robert, is buried here. The most prominent feature of the ruins is the tall square tower, with its shapely broach spire. The lower part of the tower exhibits very early Romanesque work. There is a fine thirteenth century chancel, but of the nave and claustral buildings little or nothing remains. The surroundings of the priory are very beautiful. *Situation.* 1½ miles east of Forfar on route B 9133. O.S. 1″ map sheet 50, ref. NO 482516.

Admission. All reasonable times without charge.

Official Guide Pamphlet. 6d.

St. Orland's Stone

An upstanding sculptured slab of the Early Christian period: on one side a cross in relief extending from the top to bottom; on either side of the cross shaft and upon the shaft and arms a variety of interlaced patterns executed in low relief. On the other side is an assemblage of figure subjects.

Situation. In a field near the farmhouse of Cossans 1½ miles north-east of Glamis railway station and 3½ miles west of Forfar. O.S. 1″ map sheet 50, ref. NO 401500.

Admission. All times without charge.

★St. Vigeans Museum

St. Fechin was an Irish saint who died in 644 A.D. The name St. Vigeans commemorates him, and around the church dedicated to him were buried the Picts who lived in the district. Their surviving gravestones form one of most important groups of early Christian sculpture in Scotland. These stones are now displayed in a cottage museum adjacent to the present parish church, which stands on the site of the original foundation. Besides the early Christian stones, the museum houses a number of architectural fragments from the medieval church.

Situation. In the village of St. Vigeans, 1½ miles north of the centre of Arbroath. O.S. 1″ map sheet 50, ref. NO 639429.

Hours of Admission. Standard, but closed on Sundays. Notice posted when keyholder is absent.

Admission Fee. 1s.

Official Guide Book. Early Christian and Pictish Monuments of Scotland, 5s.

Tealing Dovecot

A good example of a late sixteenth century dovecot.

Tealing Earth-house

A well preserved example of a souterrain or earth-house comprising a passage and long curved gallery and small inner chamber; Iron Age.

Situation. 5 miles north of Dundee off Dundee–Forfar road (A. 929). O.S. 1″ map sheet 50, ref. NO 413382.

Admission. All times without charge.

ARGYLL

Achnabreck

The exposed crest of a rocky ridge covered with well preserved cup-and-ring engravings of the Bronze Age.

Situation. 1½ miles north of Lochgilphead. O.S. 1″ map sheet 52, ref. NR 856906.

Admission. All times without charge.

Ardchattan Priory

One of the three Valliscaulian houses founded in Scotland in 1230 (see under Beauly, infra.). The remains are much mixed up with a modern mansion house, but include some vigorous First Pointed work, also several monuments in the characteristic late West Highland style. The priory was burned by Cromwell's soldiery in 1654.

Situation. On the north side of Loch Etive, 7 miles north-east of Oban. O.S. 1″ map sheet 46, ref. NM 971349.

Admission. All times without charge.

Ballygowan

Cup-and-ring engravings on natural rock faces; early second millennium B.C.

Situation. 1½ miles south-west of Kilmartin, towards Poltalloch. O.S. 1″ map sheet 52, ref. NR 820974.

Admission. All times without charge.

Baluachraig

Several groups of cup-and-ring engravings on natural rock faces.

Situation. 1¼ miles south of Kilmartin. O.S. 1″ map sheet 52, ref. NR 832971.

Admission. All times without charge.

Cairnbaan

A group of cup-and-ring engravings on a natural rock surface.

Situation. 300 yards north-north-west of the Cairnbaan Hotel, 2½ miles north-west of Lochgilphead. O.S. 1″ map sheet 52, ref. NR 838910.

Admission. All times without charge.

Carnasserie Castle

This very attractive castle was the house of John Carswell, first Protestant Bishop of the Isles, who translated Knox's *Liturgy* into Gaelic, and published it in 1567. It was the first book printed in that language. The castle was captured and partly blown up during Argyll's rebellion in 1685. It consists of a tower-house with a hall-house attached, but the whole building is of one date and design. Its architectural details are unusually fine for a West Highland castle.

Situation. 1¼ miles north of Kilmartin. O.S. 1″ map sheet 52, ref. NM 838009.

Admission. All times without charge.

Castle Sween

This lonely ruin, situated on the rocky western coast of Knapdale, is of high architectural importance, since it appears to be, typologically considered, one of the earliest stone castles in Scotland. It was probably built in the mid-twelfth century, and the main structure is of Norman aspect, with large pilaster and angle buttresses. A great oblong tower-house, with pointed loopholes, and a cylindrical angle tower, are later additions. The castle was destroyed by Sir Alexander Macdonald in 1647.

Situation. On the east shore of Loch Sween, in South Knapdale. O.S. 1″ map sheet 58, ref. NR 713789.

Admission. All times without charge.

Dunadd Fort

A well preserved Dark Age hill-fort with walled enclosures, identified as the capital of Dalriada, the Kingdom of the Scots.

Situation. 1½ miles west of Kilmichael Glassary, off Lochgilphead–Kilmartin road (A 816). O.S. 1″ map sheet 52, ref. NR 837936.
Admission. All times without charge.

Dunchraigaig

A denuded Bronze Age cairn; originally covered three burial cists containing inhumed and cremated human bones.
Situation. 1¼ miles south of Kilmartin, on Lochgilphead road (A 816). O.S. 1″ map sheet 52, ref. NR 833968.
Admission. All times without charge.

Dunstaffnage Castle

An exceptionally fine and well preserved example of a thirteenth century castle of *enceinte*, built on a rock, and showing the usual great curtain wall and round towers. Close beside it is a ruined chapel in a very rich First Pointed style, showing exceptional refinement and beauty in its architectural detail. The castle has a long and colourful history extending from the War of Independence to the "Forty-Five". Traditionally Dunstaffnage is the site of an early seat of the Dalriadic Kings, and it is said that the Stone of Destiny was kept there before its removal to Scone.
Situation. On the south shore of Loch Etive, 3 miles north-north-east of Oban. O.S. 1″ map sheet 46, ref. NM 883345.
Admission. Closed to the public; may be viewed from the outside only.

Eileach an Naoimh

An island with a most interesting group of Celtic monastic remains. It is intimately associated in local tradition with St. Columba. The remains include beehive cells, a chapel, and a graveyard.
Situation. One of the Garvellach Isles, in the Firth of Lorne. O.S. 1″ map sheet 52, ref. NM 668119.
Admission. All times without charge; by privately hired motor boat from Cullipool or Easdale. Enquiries to the keykeeper: Telephone: Luing 212.

Eilean Mor: St. Cormac's Chapel

This chapel consists of nave and chancel, the latter vaulted, and entered by a round arch. It contains the effigy of an ecclesiastic.
Situation. On an island off the coast of Knapdale. O.S. 1″ map sheet 58, ref. NR 666754.
Admission. All times without charge; access is difficult; by privately hired motor-boat.

Inchkenneth Chapel

A unicameral chapel of the West Highland type, with pointed windows. The burial ground contains several interesting medieval monuments, including the figure of a mailed warrior.
Situation. On the island of Inchkenneth, in Loch na Keal, on the west side of Mull. O.S. 1″ map sheet 45, ref. NM 438355.
Admission. All reasonable times without charge on application to custodian; by privately hired motor-boat.

Iona: Maclean's Cross

A fine fifteenth century free standing cross of the Hebridean type, on the road from the village to the Cathedral. It displays a Crucifixion and foliaceous interlaced work. The cross is said to commemorate a Maclean of Duart.
Situation. On the island of Iona, by the roadside between the village and the abbey. O.S. 1″ map sheet 51, ref. NM 284243.
Admission. All times without charge.

Kilberry Sculptured Stones

A collection of late medieval sculptured stones from the Kilberry estate.
Situation. Kilberry Castle, 17 miles south-south-west of Lochgilphead on the west coast of Knapdale. O.S. 1″ map sheet 58, ref. NR 710643.
Admission. All times without charge.

Kilchurn Castle

This castle dates from the middle of the fifteenth century when it was built by Sir Colin Campbell of Glenorchy, the founder of the Breadalbane family. It stands prominently in a marsh at the end of Loch Awe, in a situation of great natural beauty. The oldest part of the castle is a high, square tower. The additional buildings, erected in 1693, converted this once free standing tower into a castle surrounding an irregular courtyard.
Situation. At the north-east end of Loch Awe, 2 miles west of Dalmally; clearly visible from the main road. O.S. 1″ map sheet 53, ref. NN 133276.
Admission. Not open to the public. May be viewed from outside.

Kilmartin: Churchyard Crosses and Sculptured Stones

In this typical West Highland churchyard are preserved a number of grave slabs and fragments of at least two crosses, one showing Christ crucified on the front and Christ in Majesty on the back. The former figure is carved with exceptional refinement and feeling. The cross dates from the sixteenth century.
Situation. In Kilmartin churchyard. O.S. 1″ map sheet 52, ref. NR 835988.
Admission. All times without charge.

Kilmartin: Glebe Cairn

When excavated in 1864 the cairn, built entirely of stones, was found to contain two cists. One cist was lined with boulders and covered by a slab; the second was made entirely of slabs. This latter contained a beaker and a necklace of jet beads. Early second millennium B.C.
Situation. Kilmartin Glebe. O.S. 1″ map sheet 52, ref. NR 833989.
Admission. All times without charge.

Kilmichael Glassary

Cup-and-ring engravings of *c.* 2000–1500 B.C. on natural rock outcrop.
Situation. 3½ miles north of Lochgilphead. O.S. 1″ map sheet 52, ref. NR 858935.
Admission. All times without charge.

Kilmory Knap: Chapel

A typical small church of the West Highlands, unicameral and with a pair of round arched east windows. There is an assemblage of late medieval sculptured stones in the chapel and in the kirkyard Macmillan's Cross.

Situation. In South Knapdale, on the shore between Loch Sween and Loch Caolisport. O.S. 1" map sheet 58, ref. NR 703753.

Admission. All times without charge.

Nether Largie Cairns:
North Cairn

The northernmost of three cairns erected at the side of an ancient trackway and covering a central burial cist with large capstone bearing cup marks and representations of flat copper axe heads; *c.* 1800–1600 B.C.

Mid Cairn

A despoiled cairn, one of a line of three built at the side of an ancient trackway, and originally containing two burial cists constructed of stone slabs, grooved and adorned with cup-and-ring marks; *c.* 1800–1500 B.C.

South Cairn

A fine example of a megalithic chambered cairn of the Clyde type with segmented cist. The long narrow cist is well preserved, dating back to the third millennium B.C.

Situation. ½ mile south-west of Kilmartin. O.S. 1" map sheet 52, ref. NR 832985, 831984 and 829980.

Admission. All times without charge. Key for the North Cairn hangs on door of cairn.

Ri Cruin Cairn

A despoiled burial cairn of the Bronze Age originally covering three stone cists. Axe figures are engraved on one of the cist slabs.

Situation. 1 mile south-south-west of Kilmartin. O.S. 1" map sheet 52, ref. NR 825972.

Admission. All times without charge.

Temple Wood Stone Circle

A circle of upright stones, now much reduced in number, with a burial cist at the centre; probably early second millennium B.C.

Situation. ¾ mile south-west of Kilmartin. O.S. 1" map sheet 52, ref. NR 826979.

Admission. All times without charge.

AYRSHIRE

Crossraguel Abbey (Plate 10)

A Cluniac monastery founded by Duncan, Earl of Carrick, in 1244, as a subordinate house of Paisley. It was much patronized by the Bruces, and by the early Stewart monarchs. A famous event in its history is the roasting of

Abbot Stewart, in 1570, by the Earl of Cassillis, with the object of forcing him to surrender his title deeds. The remains of the abbey are very extensive and of high architectural distinction. They consist of the church, claustral buildings, outer court with an imposing castellated gatehouse, and abbot's house with a strong tower attached. The choir of the church, with its three-sided apse, is a fine specimen of the latest phase in Scottish Gothic, and the sacristy and chapter-house, of the same late date, are likewise very fine.

Situation. 2 miles from Maybole on the main Maybole–Girvan road (A 77). O.S. 1″ map sheet 72, ref. NS 275083.

Hours of Admission. Standard.

Admission Fee. 1s.

Card Guide. 2d.

Dundonald Castle

King Robert II, the first Stuart King, rebuilt this castle, which became his favourite residence. He died here in 1390. The king's chief work at Dundonald consists of a very large oblong tower-house, remarkable in itself and for the way in which it incorporates the remains of a 13th century gatehouse. Most of this tower, and much of the barmkin wall survive. The castle stands on an isolated hill and is a notable landmark.

Situation. At Dundonald, 4½ miles south-west of Kilmarnock off main road to Troon (A 759). O.S. 1″ map sheet 67, ref. NS 363345.

Admission. Not yet open to the public. May be viewed from the outside.

Loch Doon Castle

This castle now stands upon the shores of Loch Doon where it was transplanted some years ago from its original site in the middle of the loch on the consequence of the raising of the water level. The earliest records of the castle date it to the early fourteenth century. Its plan is unusual. The castle consists of a great curtain wall of eleven unequal sides. The walls vary in thickness from 7 feet to 9 feet and stand about 26 feet high. The masonry is of the most excellent kind. The main entrance consists of a fine pointed doorway of late thirteenth century or early fourteenth century character. It was defended by a portcullis.

Situation. 7 miles south of Dalmellington. O.S. 1″ map sheet 67, ref. NX 484950.

Admission. All times without charge.

Maybole Collegiate Church

The roofless ruin of a fifteenth century church, built for a small college established here in 1373 by the Kennedies of Dunure. The remains include a rich door in a revived First Pointed style, and an Easter Sepulchre which is also an imitation of early work.

Situation. In Maybole, south of main road (A 77). O.S. 1″ map sheet 72, ref. NS 301099.

Admission. Not yet open to the public; visible from the street.

Rowallan Castle

This house is a fine specimen of a superior Scottish mansion of the sixteenth and seventeenth centuries. It is distinguished architecturally by two imposing round towers with conical roofs which flank the entrance at first floor level. The outer entrance to the castle forecourt is through a fine sculptured doorway in the Renaissance style. The castle has a very pleasant situation in a well-timbered park on the banks of the Carmel stream.

Situation. In the Rowallan estate, about 3 miles north of Kilmarnock. O.S. 1" map sheet 60, ref. NS 435424.

Admission. Not yet open to the public. May be viewed from outside.

Skelmorlie Aisle, Largs (Plate 24)

A splendid example of a Renaissance monument: erected by Sir Robert Montgomery of Skelmorlie in 1636. The monument stands in an aisle, formerly the north transept of the old church of Largs, and is the only portion now preserved. The roof of the aisle is a timber barrel-vault divided into compartments with painted ribs imitating a rib-vaulted roof. Within the panels are painted scenes representing the Seasons, Largs Church, emblematical subjects, signs of the Zodiac and heraldic devices. The monument, which is built in stone, consists of a gallery raised above a partially sunk burial vault. The whole effect is extremely rich.

Another monument in the same art style, though greatly inferior, is built against the south wall on the outside, to the memory of the Boyles of Kelburn.

Situation. In the old churchyard north of the main road (A 78) in the centre of Largs. O.S. 1" map sheet 59, ref. NS 203595.

Admission. April–September. Standard, but notice posted when keyholder absent.

Admission Fee. 1s.

BANFFSHIRE

Auchindoun Castle

A massive ruin grandly situated on the summit of an isolated hill, enclosed by prehistoric earthworks. The central tower was built by the master mason, Thomas Cochran, the ill-starred favourite of James III. It had a groin-vaulted hall, the ribs of which were wrongly set out, so that a new start had to be made, but the difficulty was overcome in a most effective and picturesque manner. In Queen Mary's wars this was the stronghold of the redoubtable "Edom o' Gordon". The courtyard buildings were probably erected by him. Here the Jacobite leaders held a council of war after Dundee's death at Killie-crankie.

Situation. In Glen Fiddich, 2 miles south-east of Dufftown. O.S. 1" map sheet 29, ref. NJ 349375.

Admission. Not open to the public, but may be viewed from outside.

Balvenie Castle

This ancient stronghold of the Comyns, visited by Edward I in 1304, belonged subsequently to the Black Douglases and the Stewart Earls of Atholl, and was visited by Queen Mary in 1562. It had a disturbed history during the wars of the seventeenth century, and was occupied by the Hanoverians in 1746. Its great enclosing curtain wall, with a rock-hewn ditch, is a work of the Comyn period, but most of the existing buildings were erected in the fifteenth and sixteenth centuries. This is one of the largest and best preserved castles in the north of Scotland. A remarkable feature is the two-leaved iron yett.

Situation. At Dufftown. O.S. 1″ map sheet 29, ref. NJ 326408.
Hours of Admission. Standard.
Admission Fee. 1s.
Official Guide Pamphlet. 6d.

Deskford Church

This ruined building possesses a rich sacrament house, of the type peculiar
to the north-east of Scotland during the early sixteenth century (*c.f.* Kinkell).
It bears an inscription telling that "this present lovable work of sacrament
house" was provided by Alexander Ogilvy of Deskford in 1551.
Situation. 4 miles south of Cullen on route B 9018. O.S. 1″ map sheet 30,
ref. NJ 509617.
Admission. All times without charge.

Duff House

William Adam was commissioned by William Duff (later Earl of Fife) to
design Duff House in 1730. The main block was roofed in 1739 but proposed
wings were never built. Although incomplete, Adam's splendid and richly
detailed mansion is among the finest works of Georgian baroque architecture
in Britain.
Situation. ½ mile south of Banff, access from bypass south of the burgh. O.S.
1″ map sheet 30, ref. NJ 634692.
Admission. Not yet open to the public. May be viewed from outside.

BERWICK-UPON-TWEED (NORTHUMBERLAND)

Berwick was fortified with walls and a strong castle after capture by Edward I
in 1296; the defences were strengthened in the subsequent disturbed history
of the town, and finally remodelled by Elizabeth in 1558–69. The town long
continued as a strategic centre: after the 1715 rebellion a barrracks was built
to hold the garrison and after 1745 the ramparts were repaired. Berwick is
one of the outstanding fortified towns of Europe.
Official Guide Book. The Fortifications of Berwick-upon-Tweed, 2s. 6d.

Berwick Castle

Most of the medieval castle was destroyed by George Stephenson's railway,
but the north-west defences survive with added Henry VIII gun-towers.
Situation. West of railway station, access by Castle Dene park or by riverside.
Admission. Free access to riverside wall and tower, rest may be viewed from
outside.

Medieval Town Walls

The Elizabethan rebuilding took place on the landward sides of the town
inside the old north defences. The medieval walls survive along the river;
their most conspicuous remaining part to the north is the much altered Bell
Tower.
Admission. May be viewed from outside.

Elizabethan Ramparts

In 1558 the defended area was reduced and new works were built after the
latest system of artillery fortifications. The ramparts with their strong points

or bastions are preserved intact right round the landward sides of the town.
Admission. All times without charge.

Ravensdowne Barracks

The severe and monumental square of buildings erected in 1717 is one of the earliest purpose-built barracks in Britain.
Situation. The Parade.
Admission. Standard.

BERWICKSHIRE

Dryburgh Abbey (Plate 11)

One of the famous group of Border monasteries founded in the reign of David I. It was a house of Premonstratensian canons, and the founder was Hugh de Morville, Constable of Scotland. The ruins, in themselves of extreme beauty, occupy a lovely situation in a horsehoe bend of the Tweed, and are of high architectural interest because, though little save the transepts has been spared of the church itself, the claustral buildings have survived in a more complete state than in any other Scottish monastery, except Iona and Inchcolm. A great deal of the existing remains, moreover, dates from the twelfth and thirteenth centuries, though there has also been much reconstruction following on the burning of the abbey by Richard II in 1385. Both the early and the later work are marked by extreme refinement. Within the church are the graves of Sir Walter Scott and Earl Haig.
Situation. 3 miles south-east of Melrose, near St. Boswells. O.S. 1″ map sheet 70, ref. NT 591317.
Hours of Admission. Standard.
Admission Fee. 1s.
Official Guide Book. 2s. The Scottish Border Abbeys Popular Guide is also available, price 2s.

Edinshall Broch

Listed among the ten Iron Age brochs known in Lowland Scotland. Its dimensions are exceptionally large; the structure was originally defended by a series of outworks.
Situation. On the north-eastern slope of Cockburn Law, about 4 miles from Grantshouse, by the Duns road (A 6112). O.S. 1″ map sheet 63, ref. NT 773604.
Admission. All times without charge.

Edrom Church

Of the ancient and now ruined Parish Church of Edrom, there survives a Norman doorway of great beauty. Its survival is due to its incorporation and use in a burial vault erected against it. The doorway consists of a round arched opening in three orders, with angle shafts. The capitals of the shafts and the three orders of the arch are richly carved with Norman decorative details.
Situation. In Edrom, 3 miles east-north-east of Duns, off the road to Berwick-upon-Tweed (A 6105). O.S. 1″ map sheet 63, ref. NT 828558.
Admission. All times without charge.

Foulden Tithe Barn

A two-storeyed tithe barn in two floors; outside stair and crow-stepped gables. Complete.

Situation. At Foulden, 3 miles east of Chirnside on the road to Berwick-upon-Tweed (A 6105). O.S. 1″ map sheet 64, ref. NT 928556.

Admission. Not open to the public; may be viewed from the roadside.

Greenknowe Tower

A fine turreted tower-house on the L-plan, dated 1581, and still retaining its iron yett. Built by James Seton of Touch, whose armorial bearings it displays, it became in the next century the seat of Walter Pringle, the noted Covenanter.

Situation. ½ mile west of Gordon on the Earlston road (A 6105). O.S. 1″ map sheet 63, ref. NT 639428.

Admission. All reasonable times without charge, on application to custodian.

BUTE COUNTY

Auchagallon Stone Circle, Arran

A Bronze Age burial cairn surrounded by a circle of fifteen standing stones.

Situation. By the east side of a farm road 4 miles north of Blackwaterfoot. O.S. 1″ map sheet 66, ref. NR 893347.

Admission. All times without charge.

Cairn Ban, Arran

One of the most famous of the Neolithic long cairns in S.W. Scotland. From the semi-circular forecourt a gallery, now blocked by debris, ran into the cairn. The large slabs which lie adjacent formerly covered the gallery.

Situation. 3½ miles north of Kilmory on A 841 and 1 mile north of Auchareaoch Farm. O.S. 1″ map sheet 66, ref. NR 991262.

Admission. All times without charge.

Lochranza Castle, Arran

Substantial remains of what is probably a sixteenth century building sited at the extremity of a peninsula jutting out into the loch. The existence of a castle on this site is first recorded at the end of the fourteenth century.

Situation. Lochranza, Arran. O.S. 1″ map sheet 66, ref. NR 934507. Access by Clyde coast steamer.

Admission. Free on application to key-keeper, Mr. T. Kerr, Post Office, Lochranza.

Moss Farm Road Stone Circle, Arran

Remains of a Bronze Age cairn and stone circle.

Situation. South side of Moss Farm road, 3 miles north of Blackwaterfoot. O.S. 1″ map sheet 66, ref. NR 900326.

Admission. All times without charge.

*Rothesay Castle, Bute

This is one of the most remarkable and important medieval castles in Scotland. It dates from the early thirteenth century and is an outstanding example of the typical thirteenth century castle distinguished by high curtain walls fortified by projecting drum towers. The castle differs from the normal plan in that the walls enclose a circular courtyard. This plan form is unique in Scotland. The site is surrounded by a deep water moat. The entrance way is through a high tower which projects into the moat, the work of James IV and James V. Within the courtyard may be seen the foundations of sundry internal buildings, haphazardly disposed, and the roofless shell of a chapel. In all probability the castle may represent in substance that captured by the Norsemen in the year 1230.

Situation. In the centre of Rothesay. O.S. 1" map sheet 59, ref. NS 088646.
Hours of Admission. Standard.
Admission Fee. 1s.
Official Guide Pamphlet. 3d.

St. Mary's Chapel, Rothesay, Bute

Late medieval remains of the Abbey Church of St. Mary, originally the chancel, including two fine recessed and canopied tombs containing effigies of a knight in full armour, and a lady and a child.

Situation. ½ mile south of Rothesay on the A 845. O.S. 1" map sheet 59, ref. NS 086637.
Admission. Free on application to custodian at Rothesay Castle.

Torr a' Chaisteal, Arran

A former headland crowned with a circular Iron Age fort now largely buried. The entrance passage was on the east side.

Situation. 2¼ miles west of Kilmory on road A 841 near Corriecravie Farm. O.S. 1" map sheet 66, ref. NR 922233.
Admission. All times without charge.

Torrylin Cairn, Arran

A Neolithic chambered cairn of which four segments of the chamber survive. The remains of eight skeletons, a flint knife and part of a round-bottomed pot were found when the cairn was excavated in 1900.

Situation. South end of island, ½ mile south-west of Kilmory. O.S. 1" map sheet 66, ref. NR 955211.
Admission. All times without charge.

CAITHNESS

Cairn of Get

A Neolithic short-horned cairn of a type found only in this part of Scotland. The central burial chamber is entered by a passage from the S. Excavation in 1866 revealed the remains of some seven or eight skeletons as well as leaf-shaped arrowheads and pottery.

Situation. 6½ miles south-south-west of Wick and ½ mile west of A 9. O.S. 1" map sheet 16, ref. ND 314410.
Admission. All times without charge.

Castle of Old Wick

A ruined square tower of four unvaulted storeys, standing on a spine of rock projecting into the sea, between two deep narrow gulleys or geos, about one mile south of Wick. It belonged to the Cheynes, later to the Sutherlands of Duffus, and was besieged and taken by the Master of Caithness in 1569. The tower probably dates from the twelfth century.

Situation. 1 mile south of Wick on the coast half a mile east of the main road (A 9). O.S. 1″ map sheet 16, ref. ND 369489.

Admission. All times without charge, except that access prohibited when adjoining rifle range in use.

Cnoc Freiceadain

Two Neolithic long-horned cairns lying at right angles to each other on the crest of a hill. Neither has been excavated.

Situation. 1 mile north of Shebster and ¼ mile west of Shebster–Achreamie road. O.S. 1″ map sheet 11, ref. ND 012654.

Admission. All times without charge.

Grey Cairns of Camster

Two megalithic chambered cairns *c.* 3000–2000 B.C. One cairn is elongated with expanded ends or "horns" and contains two chambers. The other is round and contains a single chamber approached by a passage.

Situation. 5 miles north of Lybster, on the west side of the Lybster–Watten road. O.S. 1″ map sheet 16, ref. ND 260443.

Admission. All times without charge.

Hill o' Many Stanes

Neolithic or Bronze Age site with almost 200 stones of no great size set out in 22 parallel rows.

Situation. 3¼ miles east-north-east of Lybster and ½ mile west of road (A 9). O.S. 1″ map sheet 11, ref. ND 295384.

Admission. All times without charge.

St. Mary's Chapel, Crosskirk

A rudely-constructed chapel consisting of chancel and nave, access from one to the other being by a low and narrow doorway with inclining jambs; probably of twelfth century date. At the cliff edge nearby are the remains of a broch.

Situation. ½ mile west of Crosskirk, on the coast 6 miles west of Thurso. O.S. 1″ map sheet 11, ref. ND 025701.

Admission. All times without charge.

CLACKMANNANSHIRE

*Castle Campbell

The castle consists of a lofty oblong tower erected in the third quarter of the fifteenth century, and later buildings added in the sixteenth and seventeenth centuries. The castle is situated on the top of a rocky mound rising precipitously from the deep ravines of the beautiful Dollar Glen. From the castle a magnificent panorama over the Forth and the plains beyond is no less picturesque. The early tower is in a very good state of preservation and contains a fine stone vaulted ceiling. Fronting the courtyard in one of the later ranges is an unusual loggia of sixteenth century date.

Situation. 1 mile north of Dollar on the steep northern slope of the Ochil Hills at the head of Dollar Glen. O.S. 1″ map sheet 55, ref. NS 961993.

Hours of Admission. Standard.

Admission Fee. 1s.

Official Guide Book. 1s. 9d.

Telephone No.: 0259 4 208.

Clackmannan Tower

This interesting castle stands on a commanding site overlooking the town of Clackmannan. Before its partial collapse due to subsidence it was one of the most complete and complicated of Scottish tower-houses. It began as a fourteenth century tower, to which a "jamb" or wing was added in the next century and it is now a tall and martial edifice, embattled and turreted. From 1365 until 1772 the castle belonged to the Bruce family. It was formerly surrounded by a moat.

Situation. On the west side of Clackmannan. O.S. 1″ map sheet 55, ref. NS 906919.

Admission. No facilities for entry whilst work is in progress: may be closely viewed from the outside.

DUMFRIESSHIRE

★*Caerlaverock Castle*

The chief seat of the Maxwell family, and one of the foremost examples of medieval secular architecture in Scotland. It is famous in history and literature through its siege by Edward I in 1300, commemorated in the well-known old French poem, *Le Siege de Karlaverok*. In 1640 it was captured by the Covenanters and dismantled. The ruins, which stand within a wide moat, include much work of the thirteenth and fifteenth centuries; and the latest building, dating from 1638, is one of the finest examples of early classical Renaissance in Scotland. The shape of the castle is very remarkable, being triangular, like a shield, with a round tower at each of the two basal angles and a great gatehouse at the apex.

Situation. 7 miles south-south-east of Dumfries on the Glencaple road (B 725). O.S. 1″ map sheet 75, ref. NY 026656.

Access. Bus service from Dumfries to Glencaple; thence three miles' walk.

Hours of Admission. Standard.

Admission Fee. 1s.

Official Guide Book. 1s. 9d.

Kirkconnel Churchyard

Two gravestones, probably of seventeenth century date, can be seen in this graveyard. These traditionally mark the burials of "Fair Helen of Kirkconnel Lea" and her lover, Adam Fleming, the subjects of a traditional Scottish ballad made famous by Sir Walter Scott. The present ruined chapel and churchyard are post-Reformation, but probably stand on the site of an earlier foundation. Nearby, outside the graveyard, is a late Medieval free standing cross. Cross and church site both belong probably to the deserted Medieval village of Kirkconnel, situated adjacent.

Situation. Near Waterbeck, 1¾ miles north-east of Kirtlebridge. O.S. 1″ map sheet 75, ref. NY 250753.

Admission. At all times without charge.

*Lincluden College

In 1164 a Benedictine nunnery was founded here by Uchtred, Lord of Galloway. At the end of the fourteenth century this was suppressed by Archibald the Grim, third Earl of Douglas, who established in its place a college of eight secular canons under a provost. The existing remains are those of the collegiate church and the provost's house. The church, of which the chancel and south aisle and transept survive, dates from the early fifteenth century, and is one of the most beautiful pieces of Decorated architecture left to us in Scotland. It is remarkable for the richness of its heraldic adornment, for the noble tomb of the Princess Margaret, daughter of Robert III, and for the *pulpitum* or carved stone screen separating the chancel from the nave. The provost's house dates from the sixteenth century. Adjoining the church is a Norman *motte*, later terraced as part of a pleasance.

Situation. 1 mile north-north-west of central Dumfries, off the A 76. O.S. 1″ map sheet 74, ref. NX 997779.

Hours of Admission. Standard.

Admission Fee. 1s.

Merkland Cross

A fine fifteenth century floriated wayside cross, concerning which various legends are current locally.

Situation. In Annandale, north of the A 74, 2 miles north-west of Kirkpatrick–Fleming. O.S. 1″ map sheet 75, ref. NY 250721.

Admission. All times without charge.

Ruthwell Cross

Preserved in an annexe to the parish church, this ranks, along with the Bewcastle Cross in Cumberland, as one of the two foremost examples of Anglian sculpture, and is one of the major monuments of Dark Age Europe. The cross, which has been slightly restored, dates probably from the end of the seventh century. The main faces have figure-sculpture, mostly scriptural scenes, associated with Latin inscriptions, and on the sides are rich vine scrolls with birds and beasts. The quality of the sculpture is of the highest order. On the margins are inscribed, in runes, portions of the famous Old English poem *The Dream of the Rood*, which has been ascribed to Caedmon.

Situation. In Ruthwell Church, ½ mile north of the village and 9 miles south-east of Dumfries. O.S. 1″ map sheet 75, ref. NY 101682.

Admission. All times without charge. Key of Church must be obtained from the key-keeper, Kirkyett Cottage, Ruthwell.

DUNBARTONSHIRE

*Dumbarton Castle

Dumbarton Rock, a volcanic plug of basalt, possibly has a longer recorded history as a stronghold than any other place in Britain. From at least the fifth

E

century A.D. until 1018 it was the centre of the independent British kingdom of Strathclyde; in medieval Scotland it was an important royal castle; in more recent times Dumbarton's importance gradually declined, but it was garrisoned until the twentieth century. Dumbarton's Dark Age buildings and defences have been obliterated, and little survives from the Middle Ages. The most interesting structures are the fortifications of the seventeenth and eighteenth centuries, which illustrate a painful struggle by military engineers to adapt a problem site to contemporary defensive needs.

Situation. ½ mile south of Dumbarton East Station on the north shore of the Firth of Clyde. O.S. 1" map sheet 60, ref. NS 401744.

Admission. Standard.

Admission Fee. 1s.

Official Guide Book. 1s. 3d.

Telephone No.: 0389 2473.

EAST LOTHIAN

The Chesters

The Chesters is one of the best examples in Scotland of an Iron Age Fort with multiple ramparts. The complex earthworks are very well preserved, and there are clear remains of a considerable number of buildings in the interior. The Fort may have developed to its present form through several phases of construction.

Situation. 1 mile south of Drem. O.S. 1" map sheet 63, ref. NT 507782.

Admission. At all times without charge.

*Dirleton Castle (Plate 17)

One of the most beautiful ruins in Scotland, this ancient stronghold of the de Vaux stands amid a lovely flower-garden in the heart of the charming hamlet of Dirleton, the most English of Scottish villages. The castle had an eventful history from its first siege by Edward I in 1298 until its destruction by Lambert in 1650. The oldest work includes an imposing group of towers dating from the thirteenth century. These form, perhaps, the earliest known example of a clustered donjon. There is also much fine building of the fourteenth, fifteenth and sixteenth centuries. The castle crowns an igneous outcrop, and some of its lower chambers, including a "pit" or dungeon, are hewn out of the rock. In the garden is a seventeenth century bowling green, surrounded by ancient yews.

Situation. In the village of Dirleton on the Edinburgh–North Berwick road (A 198). O.S. 1" map sheet 63, ref. NT 516839.

Hours of Admission. Standard.

Admission Fee. 2s.

Official Guide Book. 1s. 6d.

Dunglass Collegiate Church

Founded in 1450 by Sir Alexander Hume for a provost, three chaplains, and four choir boys; consists of nave, choir, transepts, sacristy and a central tower. It is vaulted throughout, except in the tower, and the vaults, pointed in section, are covered with stone slabbed roofs. The interior embellishments are very rich. The church stands in the grounds of Dunglass House. It was held against the English in 1544, and in the eighteenth century was used as a stable.

Situation. In the Dunglass estate 1 mile north-west of Cockburnspath on the A1 between Dunbar and Berwick-upon-Tweed. O.S. 1" map sheet 63, ref. NT 767719.
Admission. All times without charge.

Haddington: St. Mary's Church

This fine cruciform church, formerly known as "the Lamp of Lothian", was the parish church of the ancient burgh of Haddington, and its nave is still so used, but the rest of the building is a ruin in the custody of the Ministry. The whole building dates from the fifteenth century and is one of the largest and noblest examples of Scottish ecclesiastical architecture of that period. The east walls of the transept and the end walls of the choir aisles are window-less, a Scottish practice of the period. The flamboyant tracery of the large windows is exceptionally forceful, and the triple windows of the lofty tower form a landmark in the countryside. During the great siege of Haddington in 1548 the church suffered much, and narrowly escaped complete destruction. Its walls are still pitted with bullet marks.
Situation. South-east outskirts of Haddington. O.S. 1" map sheet 63, ref. NT 519736.
Admission. All times without charge.

Haddington: St. Martin's Church

The ruined nave of a Romanesque church, altered in the thirteenth century when a structure was vaulted and buttresses added. The chancel has disappeared.
Situation. On the eastern outskirts of Haddington. O.S. 1" map sheet 63, ref. NT 521739.
Admission. All times without charge.

*Hailes Castle

This beautiful ruin is of exceptional interest because its oldest portions date from before the War of Independence, and represent, not so much a castle as a fortified manor-house, closely resembling the well-known Aydon Castle in Northumberland. It then belonged to the Gourlays, but afterwards passed to the Hepburns, by whom a great square tower and high curtain walls were added. There is also a fine sixteenth century chapel. The castle was heavily involved in the Rough Wooing, and was dismantled by Cromwell in 1650. It stands in a lovely situation on the bank of the Tyne.
Situation. 1½ miles south-west of East Linton. O.S. 1" map sheet 63, ref. NT 575758.
Hours of Admission. Standard.
Admission Fee. 1s.
Official Guide Pamphlet. 3d.

Ormiston Market Cross

A fine free-standing fifteenth century cross, with a blank shield of arms, now erected on a modern base in the main street of the village.
Situation. In the village of Ormiston, about 2 miles south of Tranent (B 6371). O.S. 1" map sheet 62, ref. NT 414693.
Admission. All times without charge.

Preston Market Cross

One of the two surviving Scottish market crosses of its type, and the only one that still stands where and as it was built. It is a circular structure, with niches and a parapet, within which rises a tall shaft surmounted by a unicorn. Probably it was erected by the Hamiltons of Preston after they obtained the right to hold a fair in 1617.

Situation. About ½ mile inland from the coastal town of Prestonpans, near the main Edinburgh–North Berwick road (A 198). O.S. 1″ map sheet 62, ref. NT 391741.

Admission. All times without charge.

★*Seton Collegiate Church*

One of the most important ecclesiastical monuments in the near vicinity of Edinburgh. The church comprises a choir, north and south transepts and an unusual crossing tower of the type known as a broach tower. Foundations of the nave have been revealed during excavations. The nave was probably never erected, but the choir and transepts are complete. They are vaulted in stone and the transepts are still roofed with heavy stone slabs in a manner characteristic of this period. The church dates from the late fourteenth century. The collegiate foundation consisted of a provost, six prebendaries, one clerk and two singing-boys. Within are two good mural monuments in the Renaissance manner. At the east end is a fine arched mural tomb recess with two recumbent effigies of a Lord and his Lady, commemorating probably George, third Lord Seton, who was slain at Flodden in 1513, and his wife. The monument is charmingly situated in well-wooded grounds. Nearby are the ruins of later domestic buildings.

Situation. 1 mile south-east of Cockenzie on the main Edinburgh–North Berwick road (A 198) by St. Germain's level crossing. O.S. 1″ map sheet 62, ref. NT 418751.

Hours of Admission. Standard.

Admission Fee. 1s.

★*Tantallon Castle* (Plate 20)

This famous stronghold of the Douglases occupies a magnificent situation on the rocky coast of the Firth of Forth. Its historical renown is overmatched by the romantic glamour shed upon it through the part it plays in Scott's *Marmion*. The great frontal curtain wall, flanked by round towers and having an imposing central gatehouse, dates from the fourteenth century, and is one of the grandest things of its kind in Scotland. Outside the castle are extensive earthworks, some of which represent the defences thrown up against the cannon of James V in 1526; while others, still further out, date from the Civil War.

Situation. On the coast about 3 miles east of North Berwick. O.S. 1″ map sheet 63, ref. NT 596850.

Hours of Admission. Standard.

Admission Fee. 2s.

Official Guide. 1s. 9d.

FIFE

★*Aberdour Castle*

An extensive ruin overlooking Aberdour harbour. The oldest part is a rhomboidal tower of the fourteenth century, to which other buildings have been

added by successive stages in the sixteenth and seventeenth centuries. Parts of the later buildings are still roofed. A terraced garden and bowling green may still be traced, and a fine circular dovecot remains in good preservation. Close by is the Norman parish church. King Robert Bruce granted the barony to Randolph, Earl of Moray; later it passed to the Douglases, Earls of Morton. *Situation.* In the village of Aberdour on the Firth of Forth between Inverkeithing and Burntisland (A 92). O.S. 1″ map sheet 55, ref. NT 193854.
Hours of Admission. Standard.
Admission Fee. 1s.
Official Guide Book. 1s. 9d.

*Culross Abbey

This Cistercian monastery was founded by Malcolm, Earl of Fife, in 1217. There remains of it the choir, still used as the parish church, and parts, more or less, of the nave, the cellarium, the frater and the dorter. Only the south wall of the nave belongs to the early thirteenth century; the rest of the buildings date mostly from about 1300, and were again reconstructed in the reign of James IV. The rood screens and pulpitum are of particular interest. The fine central tower, still complete, bears the arms of Abbot Masoun (1498–1513). Culross was a daughter-house of Kinloss, in Moray.
Situation. On the northern outskirts of Culross on the Firth of Forth between Kincardine and Dunfermline (A 985). O.S. 1″ map sheet 55, ref. NS 989863.
Hours of Admission. Standard, but notice posted when keyholder absent.
Admission. Without charge.
NOTE: Application to visit the church should be made at the Manse.

*Culross, The Palace

This charming mansion was built between 1597 and 1611 by George Bruce of Culross, a wealthy merchant who was knighted by James VI. Its crow-stepped gables, and pantiled roofs have long been a favourite subject with artists, while the painted ceilings are as fine as anything of their kind in Scotland. Adjoining the Palace is a terraced garden, gay with flowers.
Situation. In the village of Culross on the Firth of Forth between Kincardine and Dunfermline (A 985). O.S. 1″ map sheet 55, ref. NS 985859.
Hours of Admission. Standard.
Admission Fee. 1s.

Dogton Stone

A much battered and weathered free-standing Celtic cross, with traces of animal and figure sculpture and interlaced and key-pattern ornament.
Situation. At Dogton farmhouse, 1½ miles north-east of Cardenden and 4½ miles north-west of central Kirkcaldy. O.S. 1″ map sheet 55, ref. NT 236969.
Admission. All times without charge.

*Dunfermline Abbey

This great Benedictine house owes its foundation to Queen Margaret, and the foundations of her church remain beneath the present nave, which is a splendid piece of late Norman work, obviously by masons from Durham. The site of the choir is now occupied by a modern parish church, which is not in the care of the Ministry, but at the east end of this the remains of St. Margaret's shrine, dating from the thirteenth century, are seen. King Robert Bruce is buried in the choir, his grave marked by a modern brass. Of the monastic buildings, the ruins of the frater, kitchen, pend and guest-house still remain, and are of much beauty and interest. The guest-house was later reconstituted as a royal palace, and here Charles I was born.

Situation. In Dunfermline. O.S. 1″ map sheet 55, ref. NT 090873.

Hours of Admission to Nave. Standard, weekdays. Sundays, Summer 2 p.m.– 6 p.m. Winter 2 p.m.–4.30 p.m. Without charge.

⋆Inchcolm Abbey (Plate 14)

Sometimes described as "The Iona of the East", the remains of this monastery stand on a green island in the Firth of Forth. It was an Augustinian house, founded about 1123 by Alexander I. The monastic buildings, which include a fine thirteenth century octagonal chapter house, are the best preserved in Scotland. The nave of the church is Norman, but it was gradually extended eastward, until a complete new cruciform church took the place of the early one, which was then converted into a dwelling house. In the original choir was discovered the finest example of thirteenth century wall-painting left in Scotland, showing a funeral procession of clerics. The abbey was much harried by English fleets, and the canons were frequently obliged to flee to the mainland. West of the abbey is a fine hog-backed stone.

Situation. On an island in the Firth of Forth south of Aberdour. O.S. 1″ map sheet 62, ref. NT 190826.

Access. Local boat hirers operate from Aberdour during summer months. Details of tides may be obtained from the Abbey custodian. (2211 332).

Hours of Admission. Standard.

Admission Fee. 1s.

Official Guide Book. 1s. 6d.

Ravenscraig Castle

An imposing ruin with deep rock-cut ditch on a promontory between Dysart and Kirkcaldy. It was founded by James II in 1460, and the building accounts extending to 1463, are in part preserved. Later the castle passed into the hands of the Sinclair Earls of Orkney. It is remarkable both for the beauty of its ashlar masonry and also because it is perhaps the first British castle to be systematically designed for defence by fire-arms.

Situation. On the coast towards the north end of the royal burgh of Kirkcaldy. O.S. 1″ map sheet 56, ref. NT 291925.

Admission. Work in progress: free admission during working hours.

Rosyth Castle and Dovecot

The castle consists of a square tower of sixteenth century date and buildings now ruinous, of a later age. The castle is in a good state of preservation and comprises three chambers, one upon another, served by a corner wheel stair rising from the ground floor. The additional buildings formed a courtyard round the original free-standing tower. The ground floor and the first floor of the tower are vaulted. The dovecot has a fine stone roof and gabled ends.

Situation. In Rosyth Dockyard. O.S. 1″ map sheet 62, ref. NT 109823.

Admission. On prior application to Ministry of Public Building and Works, Argyle House, 3 Lady Lawson Street, Edinburgh EH3 9SD.

*St. Andrews Castle

This was the archiepiscopal castle of the primate of Scotland. Here Cardinal Beaton was murdered in 1546 and the first round of the Reformation struggle was fought out in the great siege that followed. The oldest parts of the extensive ruin date from the thirteenth century, but much of the work is later than the destruction of 1547. Notable features are the grim "Bottle-dungeon", and the mine and counter-mine tunnelled in the living rock during the siege. These works are unique in Britain. The castle stands on a promontory thrust out into the North Sea, and isolated by a deep and wide ditch.

Situation. On the shore in St. Andrews. O.S. 1″ map sheet 56, ref. NO 513169.
Hours of Admission. Standard.
Admission Fee. 1s. Including Bottle-dungeon and Subterranean Passage.
Official Guide Book. 1s. 3d.

*St. Andrew's Cathedral and Priory

Of the metropolitan cathedral of Scotland, once the largest church in the country, with a length of 391 feet, little now remains save parts of the east and west gables, the south wall of the nave, and portions of the choir and south transept; but the foundations of the entire church have been recovered by excavation. The outline of the claustral buildings is also distinct, and considerable portions of the eastern and southern ranges still remain. Most of the surviving work belongs to the late twelfth and thirteenth centuries. The cathedral was also the church of a Priory of Augustinian Canons Regular.

A large part of the precinct walls, including the Pends, or vaulted entrance passage, and a number of round towers, is still extant. This wall with its towers, dates from the fourteenth century (see "Precincts and Pends"). In the cathedral museum is a magnificent collection of Celtic and medieval monuments, as well as pottery, glass work and other relics discovered on the site.

Situation. In St. Andrews. O.S. 1″ map sheet 56, ref. NO 514167.
Hours of Admission Standard, without charge.
Official Guide Book. 1s. 9d. The Guide Book to Early Christian and Pictish Monuments of Scotland is also available. Price 5s.

St. Andrews: St. Rule's, or St. Regulus' Church (Plate 8)

This was the first church of the Augustinian Canons, and was built by Bishop Robert (1126–59). It is by far the most interesting Romanesque church in Scotland. The remains consist of a choir and a western tower; the sanctuary and the later nave have gone. A feature of the building is its loftiness: the tower rises to a height of 108 feet. The Romanesque detail has been shown to have been derived from the church of Wharran-le-Street, in Yorkshire.

Situation. In St. Andrews, within cathedral precincts.
Hours of Admission. Standard.
Admission Fee. 1s., including Cathedral museum.
Official Guide Book. Described in the Cathedral Guide.

St. Andrews: Precinct Wall and Pends

The precincts of the cathedral and priory of St. Andrews were some thirty acres in extent. They were enclosed by a high wall almost a mile in total length and fortified by projecting round towers disposed at intervals through-out. The precinct wall still stands about 25 feet high and is a prominent architectural feature at the east end of the town. The projecting towers are furnished with loops and carved heraldic panels, by which it has been attributed to Prior John Hepburn and his nephew and successor, Prior Patrick Hepburn, who held office in the cathedral in the sixteenth century. The "Pends" is the stately ruin of a once-vaulted gatehouse to the cathedral precincts: fourteenth century; at the west end of the cathedral.

Situation. East end of St. Andrews surrounding the cathedral; fronting the Abbey Walk, the harbour, and the cliffs on the north side.

Admission. All times without charge.

Official Guide Book. Described in the Cathedral Guide.

St. Andrews: St. Mary's Church, Kirkheugh

The scanty foundations of a small cruciform church, on the edge of the cliff behind the cathedral. It is said to have been the church of the Culdee fraternity, and was pulled down by the Reformers in 1559.

Situation. East of cathedral, outside the precinct wall.

Admission. All times without charge.

St. Andrews: Blackfriar's Chapel

An apsidal, groin-vaulted aisle, built in 1525, is all that remains of this church.

Situation. Beside South Street, St. Andrews. O.S. 1″ map sheet 56, ref. NO 507165.

Admission. All times without charge.

St. Andrews: The West Port

This is one of the few surviving examples of a city gate in Scotland. Its building contract is dated 18th May, 1589. The Port was completely renovated in 1843 when some structural alterations were made. It now consists of a central archway protected from above by battling between two semi-octagonal turrets with gun-loops. On either side across the pavements is an arch of modern construction.

Situation. Across the west end of South Street, St. Andrews. O.S. 1″ map sheet 56, ref. NO 506165.

Admission. All times without charge.

St. Bridget's Church, Dalgety

The old church forms the eastern part of the monument which has to the west a later two-storey building comprising a burial vault on the ground floor with a "laird's loft" above, from which access was obtained to a western gallery within the church. The ancient church was dedicated to St. Bridget in 1244. The walls survive but are roofless. Later buildings have also been erected against the north wall, in the Renaissance style.

Situation. On the shores of the Forth, 2 miles south-west of Aberdour. O.S. 1″ map sheet 62, ref. NT 169838.

Admission. All times without charge.

Scotstarvit Tower

This fine tower is celebrated as the residence in the seventeenth century of Sir John Scot, author of *Scot of Scotstarvit's Staggering State of Scots Statesmen*, which Carlyle described as "a homily on life's nothingness enforced by examples". On its own merits, the tower is well worth a visit. Ashlar-faced, embattled and turreted, it rises to a height of five storeys and a garret, with roof and all complete. The two main apartments are vaulted. An armorial panel is dated 1627, but the tower is known to have been in existence in 1579. *Situation.* 2 miles south of Cupar off the Cupar–Kennoway road (A 916). O.S. 1″ map sheet 56, ref. NO 370113.

Admission. All reasonable times without charge on application to custodian.

HEBRIDES: for monuments in the Hebrides see under Inverness-shire, and Ross and Cromarty.

INVERNESS-SHIRE

Beauly Priory

One of the three monastic houses of the Valliscaulian Order founded in Scotland—all in the same year, 1230. The other two were Pluscarden in Moray and Ardchattan in Argyll (see *supra*, p. 76). Nothing but the church remains above ground. It is a long narrow building, comprising an aisleless nave, transepts, and chancel. The plan is extremely interesting, as it represents the earliest form of Cistercian church in Britain. Much of the building was reconstructed in the fourteenth–sixteenth centuries, and a north chapel was added to the nave. The architecture of all periods is very beautiful. The north transept now forms the burial place of the Mackenzies of Kintail, and contains the fine monument of Sir Kenneth Mackenzie (*d.* 1541). *Situation.* In Beauly. O.S. 1″ map sheet 27, ref. NH 528466.

Hours of Admission. Standard.

Admission Fee. 1s.

Official Guide Pamphlet. 6d.

Clava Cairns

A group of burial cairns in which three concentric rings of great stones are now the principal features exposed; of late Neolithic or Early Bronze Age date. *Situation.* 5½ miles east of Inverness, on the south bank of the River Nairn, opposite Culloden battlefield. O.S. 1″ map sheet 28, ref. NH 756445.

Admission. All times without charge.

Corrimony Cairn

Megalithic chambered cairn, probably Neolithic, surrounded by a peristalith of stone slabs, outside which is a circle of 11 standing stones. Access was by a low passage to the central circular chamber which contained a single crouched burial. *Situation.* Glen Urquhart, 8 miles west of Drumnadrochit. O.S. 1″ map sheet 27, ref. NH 383303.

Admission. All times without charge.

*Fort George

Fort George was begun in 1748 as a result of the Jacobite rebellion. An immensely strong fortification was constructed as a Government strong point to guard against any future rising. The bastioned fort and its outworks have survived almost unaltered since they were built, and Fort George is one of the finest late artillery fortifications in Europe.

The interior contains the regimental museum of the Queen's Own Highlanders.

Situation. 8½ miles north-east of Inverness, 6½ miles west of Nairn. O.S. 1″ map sheet 28, ref. NH 762567.

Hours of Admission. Standard.

Admission Fee. 1s.

Official Guide Pamphlet. Available.

Glenelg Brochs: Dun Telve and Dun Troddan

Two Iron Age broch towers, ruinous but with wall portions still standing over 30 feet in height. Entrances, galleries, courts and other structural features well preserved.

Situation. On the west coast of Inverness-shire about 1½ miles south-east of Glenelg which is 8 miles west of Shiel Bridge. O.S. 1″ map sheet 35, ref. NG 829172 and 834172.

Admission. All times without charge.

Inverlochy Castle

A fine and well preserved example of a thirteenth century castle of the Comyns, with a quadrangular wall and round angle towers displaying the characteristic long bow-slits of the period. One of the towers, larger than the rest, forms the donjon. The castle has an eventful history dating from the War of Independence and was the scene of Montrose's great victory over the Campbells on 2nd February, 1645.

Situation. 1½ miles north-east of Fort William and 1½ miles south-west of modern castle. O.S. 1″ map sheet 35, ref. NN 121755.

Admission. Not yet open to the public. May be viewed from outside.

Knocknagael Boar Stone

A roughly shaped slab. At the top is incised the mirror-case symbol and below the figure of a boar.

Situation. On Knocknagael farm, beside a secondary road, about 2½ miles south-south-west of Inverness railway station. O.S. 1″ map sheet 28, ref. NH 657413.

Admission. All times without charge.

Rodel: St. Clement's Church

The only cruciform medieval church in the Outer Isles. It was built by Alasdair Crottach MacLeod, eighth chief of Dunvegan Castle, in Skye, and contains his stately tomb, in which he was buried in 1547. The rich decoration of the church has obviously been derived from the work at Iona, and like the latter, betrays strong Irish influence. Some fine grave slabs of the late West Highland pattern may be seen in the churchyard.

Situation. Rodel, at the south end of the Isle of Harris. O.S. 1″ map sheet 17, ref. NG 047832.
Admission. All reasonable times without charge on application to custodian.

Ruthven Barracks

Ruthven Barracks were built in 1719 to check Jacobite disaffection. They were designed to hold a company in two blocks enclosed by a loopholed wall flanked by towers. A stable to the west was added by order of General Wade in 1728. The barracks were captured and burnt by Prince Charles Edward in 1746. They were never re-occupied.
Situation. ¾ mile south-east of Kingussie, access from B 970. O.S. 1″ map sheet 37, ref. NN 765997.
Admission. All times without charge.

*Urquhart Castle

One of the largest castles in Scotland, this extensive ruin occupies a commanding situation on a promontory jutting forth into Loch Ness, and must have been even more imposing before the level of the water was raised. Occupying the site of a vitrified fort, the castle began as a *motte* with a double bailey, the defences of which were rehabilitated in stone during the fourteenth century. Most of the existing buildings, however, including the gate-house and the upper part of the great square tower, date from after the Chiefs of Grant got possession of the castle in 1509. It has played a great part in Scottish history from the invasion of Edward I until the Jacobite rising of 1689, after which it was blown up.
Situation. On the west shore of Loch Ness, 1½ miles south-east of Drumnadrochit. O.S. 1″ map sheet 27, ref. NH 531286.
Hours of Admission. Standard.
Admission Fee. 1s.
Official Guide. 1s. 6d.

KINROSS-SHIRE

Burleigh Castle

A fine tower-house dating from about 1500, roofless but otherwise almost intact, to which there is still attached the fore-curtain of the barmkin or courtyard enclosure with an entrance flanked by gun-loops, and a picturesque angle tower, corbelled out above with a square cap-house, still roofed. The cap-house is dated 1582. This was the seat of the ancient family of Balfour of Burleigh. The castle was several times visited by James VI.
Situation. ½ mile east of Milnathort on the Leslie road (A 911). O.S. 1″ map sheet 55, ref. NO 130047.
Admission. All reasonable times without charge on application to key-keeper at farm opposite.

*Loch Leven Castle

Consists of a tower of late fourteenth or early fifteenth century date standing on one side of an irregular courtyard enclosed by a curtain wall of later date, probably sixteenth century. This curtain, however, embodies some older masonry, probably of the castle besieged by the English in 1325. At one angle of the curtain is a projecting circular four-storeyed tower with gun-loops. The tower is oblong on plan and contains five storeys.

Mary Queen of Scots was imprisoned in the castle in 1567 and from it escaped a year later.

The Castle can be seen across the waters of the Loch from the main Edinburgh–Perth road, before entering Kinross.

Situation. On an island in Loch Leven. O.S. 1″ map sheet 55, ref. NO 138018.

Admission. Kinross Town Council ferry service: Adult 2s. 6d., child 1s. (under 14 years of age). Free admission to castle.

Daily in summer only except Sundays—10 a.m.–6 p.m.

  Sundays—2 p.m.–6 p.m.

KIRKCUDBRIGHTSHIRE

*Cardoness Castle

This ancient home of the McCullochs stands on a rocky platform above the Water of Fleet. It is a fine and well-preserved fifteenth century tower-house, four storeys in height, with a vaulted basement. The fireplaces in the great hall and the upper hall or solar are particularly good. Remains of outer defences still exist.

Situation. 1 mile south-west of Gatehouse of Fleet on the main road to Newton Stewart (A 75). O.S. 1″ map sheet 73, ref. NX 591553.

Hours of Admission. Standard.

Admission Fee. 1s.

Cairn Holy

Two cairns which belong to the Galloway group of Clyde–Carlingford chambered tombs. The entrances had been blocked by large stones which subsequently fell or were pulled forward. Excavations showed that the earlier usage was associated with Neolithic pottery and that there was a second phase represented by the presence of Beaker fragments (*c.* 1800 B.C.).

Situation. 4 miles south-east of Creetown off the road to Gatehouse of Fleet (A 75). O.S. 1″ map sheet 80, ref. NX 518541.

Admission. All times without charge.

Carsluith Castle

A roofless sixteenth century tower-house on the L-plan, which differs from most buildings of this class in that the staircase wing or "jamb" is an addition, dated 1568. The original square tower had an open parapet with angle turrets. This castle belonged to the Browns of Carsluith, and one of its owners was the last abbot of Sweetheart Abbey.

Situation. 3 miles south-south-east of Creetown on the road to Gatehouse of Fleet (A 75). O.S. 1″ map sheet 80, ref. NX 495542.

Admission. All reasonable times without charge, on application to custodian.

Drumcoltran Tower

The building is oblong on plan, three storeys high with a garret storey in the roof, all served by a wheel or spiral stair in a projecting square stair tower or wing: a good example of a Scottish tower house of about the middle of the sixteenth century. It is simple and severe; has a slightly overhanging parapet wall supported on projecting corbels. The gables of the typical saddle-backed roof are set back from the parapet wall.

Situation. Among farm buildings, 4½ miles north-east of Dalbeattie, west of the Dumfries road (A 711). O.S. 1″ map sheet 81, ref. NX 869683.

Admission. All times without charge.

*Dundrennan Abbey

This Cistercian house was founded by David I and Fergus, Lord of Galloway, in 1142, and was colonized from Rievaulx. Here Mary Queen of Scots spent her last night on her native soil, before seeking shelter in England. The ruins, which are considerable and of great beauty, include much late Norman and Transitional work, and a rich chapter-house dating from the end of the thirteenth century. Of the church, little but the west end and the transepts now remains. The western claustral range is fairly well preserved, but of the southern little remains. Among the ruins are preserved many fine monuments, including a rather gruesome one of an abbot who had been murdered, possibly by a native Gallovidian who disliked the incoming Latin monks.

Situation. Dundrennan, 6½ miles south-east of Kirkcudbright. O.S. 1″ map sheet 81, ref. NX 749475.

Hours of Admission. Standard.

Admission Fee. 1s.

Official Guide Pamphlet. 3d.

*Maclellan's Castle, Kirkcudbright

This handsome castellated mansion was built after 1577 by Sir Thomas Maclellan of Bombie, it is said out of the stones of the Greyfriars convent in Kirkcudbright. A heraldic group over the door bears the date 1582. The house is elaborately planned, and its architectural details are particularly fine. It has been a ruin since 1752. Its builder was Provost of Kirkcudbright, and his fine late Gothic or early Renaissance altar tomb remains in the Old Greyfriars Kirk.

Situation. In the centre of Kirkcudbright. O.S. 1″ map sheet 80, ref. NX 683551.

Hours of Admission. Standard.

Admission Fee. 1s.

*Orchardton Tower

An example, unique in Scotland, of a tower house of cylindrical form. It was built by John Cairns about the middle of the fifteenth century, and in other aspects its arrangements do not differ from those of the normal rectangular tower-houses of that time. The first floor room served both as hall and chapel. There are some remnants of outbuildings.

Situation. At Old Orchardton, 5½ miles south-east of Castle Douglas. O.S. 1″ map sheet 81, ref. NX 817551.

Admission. All reasonable times without charge on application to custodian.

*Sweetheart Abbey (Plate 13)

One of the most beautiful monastic ruins in Scotland, and famous because of the touching circumstances of its foundation, by Dervorgilla, Lady of

Galloway, in memory of her husband, John Balliol, the founder of Balliol College, Oxford. The foundation dates from 1273, and in 1289 the foundress was buried in front of the high altar, with the "sweet heart" of her lord resting on her bosom. The monks were Cistercians, brought from Dundrennan. A remarkable feature of the ruins is the well-preserved precinct wall, enclosing 30 acres, and built of enormous boulders—no doubt cleared off the ground by the monks when they prepared the site for their convent. Little remains but the church, whose central tower is a conspicuous landmark. Much of the work dates from the early fourteenth century.

Situation. At New Abbey, 6 miles south of Dumfries on the coast road (A 710). O.S. 1″ map sheet 74, ref. NX 965663.
Hours of Admission. Standard.
Admission Fee. 1s.
Official Guide Book. 1s. 9d.

★*Threave Castle*

This mighty tower of the "Black Douglases" stands on a lonely islet in the River Dee. It was built towards the end of the fourteenth century by Archibald the Grim, third Earl of Douglas and Lord of Galloway. The tower, which is four storeys high, is enclosed by an outer wall, with round towers loop-holed for firearms. This dates from 1513, in the crisis that followed Flodden. The castle was dismantled after its capture by the Covenanters in 1640.

Situation. 1½ miles west of Castle Douglas. Access by farm road from road to Gatehouse of Fleet (A 75). O.S. 1″ map sheet 81, ref. NX 739623.
Hours of Admission. Open April to September. Standard, but closed on Thursdays.
Admission Fee. 1s. (includes ferry charge).
Official Guide Pamphlet. 6d.

LANARKSHIRE

★*Bothwell Castle* (Plate 18)

This was the largest and finest stone castle in Scotland dating from before the War of Independence, though the full design seems never to have been completed. It was the principal English base in western Scotland during the Plantagenet occupation, and was repeatedly taken and retaken. The chief remnant of the original structure is the superb cylindrical donjon, one half of which was cast down by the Scots when they finally retook the castle in 1336. Later it belonged to the Douglases, to whom its reconstruction is due. The Douglas buildings include a hall and a chapel, both in very rich architecture. The castle is grandly situated on a steep bank overlooking a bend of the River Clyde, and stands in a spacious and well-timbered park. Near it are the fifteenth century Bothwell Church and Bothwell Bridge, where the Covenanters were defeated by Monmouth in 1679.

Situation. ¾ mile south-west of Uddingston. O.S. 1″ map sheet 60, ref. NS 688593.
Hours of Admission. Standard.
Admission Fee. 1s.
Official Guide Book. 1s. 6d.

Coulter Motte Hill

A good example of an early medieval castle mound, originally moated and probably surmounted by a palisade enclosing a timber tower.
Situation. At Coulter railway station. O.S. 1″ map sheet 68, ref. NT 019363.
Admission. All times without charge.

Craignethan Castle

This extensive and well-preserved ruin, famous as the "Tillietudlem" of Scott's *Old Mortality*, has a history of much importance in the religious wars of the sixteenth century, when, as chief stronghold of the Hamiltons, supporters of Queen Mary, it was repeatedly assailed by the Protestant party, and partly dismantled by them in 1579. The oldest and central portion is a large tower house of an unusual design, and very ornate in its details. This was built by Sir James Hamilton of Finnart, the favourite of James V. The outer walls and towers are exceptionally well preserved.
Situation. 4½ miles west-north-west of Lanark, on the west bank of the River Nethan. O.S. 1″ map sheet 61, ref. NS 815463.
Hours of Admission. Standard.
Admission Fee. 1s.

*Crookston Castle

Substantial remains of early fifteenth century tower of unusual type within the ditch and bank of a medieval earthwork. The castle takes its name from Sir Robert Croc of Neilston, a vassal of the Steward of Scotland in the twelfth century. In the fourteenth the lands passed to Alan Stewart of Darnley, cousin of Robert II, whose descendants included Sir John Stewart, Constable of the Scots in France, who was killed at the siege of Orleans in 1429 and was probably the builder of the tower.
Situation. 1 mile south-east of Crookston and 2¾ miles east-south-east of Paisley. O.S. 1″ map sheet 60, ref. NS 525627.
Hours of Admission. Standard.
Admission Fee. 1s.
Official Guide Book. In preparation.

*Glasgow Cathedral (Plate 9)

The most complete medieval cathedral surviving on the Scottish mainland. It is remarkable for the ambulatory that runs all round the building, thus providing for the traffic of pilgrims to the shrine of St. Mungo (Kentigern), placed in a crypt or lower church under the eastern limb, where the ground falls. The cathedral comprises an aisled nave, aisled choir and presbytery, dwarf transepts and a central tower crowned with a lofty stone spire. The two western towers have unhappily been removed. Externally the great church seems somewhat austere, but this is amply compensated by the glories of the interior. The presbytery dates from the thirteenth century, the nave was built about 1300, and the tower a century later. In 1484 the Blacader aisle was attached to the south transept. Notable features in this splendid building are the elaborate vaulting in the crypt, the fourteenth century timber roof, and the stone screen or pulpitum of the fifteenth century. At the north east corner is the sacristy, completed in the fifteenth century in the manner of a castle.

Situation. In Cathedral Square, off Castle Street, Glasgow. O.S. 1″ map sheet 60, ref. NS 603656.

Admission. Weekdays	April–May	10 a.m.—6 p.m.
	June–Sept.	10 a.m.—7 p.m.
	Oct.–March	10 a.m.—5 p.m.
Sundays		1 p.m.—6 p.m.

Without charge.

St. Bride's Church, Douglas

All that remains of this church is the unaisled choir and the south side of the nave. The choir contains three fine altar-tombs of the great Douglas family, whose principal shrine this was. These monuments, which, with the choir' itself, have been restored, commemorate the "Good Sir James", Bruce's paladin; Archibald, fifth Earl of Douglas and "James the Gross", seventh Earl, with his lady. Some loose fragments of the pre-existing Norman church are extant.

Situation. In Douglas, on the Edinburgh–Cumnock road (A 70). O.S. 1″ map sheet 68, ref. NS 835311.

Admission. All reasonable times without charge, on application to custodian.

MIDLOTHIAN

Castle Law Fort

A small Iron Age hill fort consisting of two concentric banks and ditches. In the older rock-cut ditch a souterrain or earth-house is preserved. The site was occupied into Roman times (second century A.D.).

Situation. On the summit of Castle Knowe, a small hill on the south-eastern slopes of the Pentland Hills west of the Edinburgh–Carlops road (A 702) about 1 mile north-west of Glencorse. O.S. 1″ map sheet 62, ref. NT 229639.

Admission. Without charge. May be viewed from outside. Permission to enter by prior application only to the Ministry of Public Building and Works, Argyle House, 3 Lady Lawson Street, Edinburgh EH3 9SD.

*Crichton Castle

One of the largest and finest of Scottish castles, standing on a bare and lofty site overlooking the River Tyne. The nucleus is a plain fourteenth century tower-house, to which a group of buildings, dating variously from the fifteenth–seventeenth centuries, has been added, so as to form a quadrangular mansion, enclosing a narrow courtyard. The most spectacular feature of these additions is an arcaded range, the upper frontage of which is wrought with faceted stone work.

This work, in the Italianate manner, was erected by the Earl of Bothwell between 1581 and 1591. He had been in Italy, and probably had seen the Palazzo dei Diamanti at Ferrara. Near the castle is the fine fifteenth century parish church.

Situation. 2¼ miles south-south-west of Pathhead which is on the Edinburgh–Lauder road (A 68). O.S. 1″ map sheet 62, ref. NT 380612.

Hours of Admission. Standard; but closed on Fridays, October to May.

Admission Fee. 1s.

Official Guide Book. 1s. 3d.

*Edinburgh Castle

The most famous of Scottish castles, and now additionally celebrated because it contains the Scottish National Memorial of the First World War. The walls which enclose the summit of the mighty basalt rock retain some medieval work, but mostly belong to the seventeenth and eighteenth centuries: the Half Moon Battery was built by the Regent Morton, and encloses the remains of the great tower built by David II and destroyed by English guns in the siege of 1573. The oldest building on the rock is St. Margaret's Chapel, a small example of Norman work. The Great Hall, built by James IV, retains its fine open timber roof. The royal apartments still show some of their painted decoration. Here are preserved the Regalia or crown jewels of Scotland. In front of St. Margaret's Chapel stands the famous fifteenth century bombard, Mons Meg.

Situation. Centre of Edinburgh. O.S. 1″ map sheet 62, ref. NT 252736.
Hours of Admission:
Summer Hours (June–September inclusive), subject to Military Tattoo requirements:

Week-days	9.30 a.m.—6 p.m.	(All apartments.)
	6.00 p.m.—9 p.m.	(Precincts only.)
Sundays	11.00 a.m.—6 p.m.	(All apartments.)
	6.00 p.m.—9 p.m.	(Precincts only.)

Hours are slightly shorter at other times of the year and details may be obtained by telephoning the number below.

Admission Fee. 2s. in Winter 3s. in Summer (children 1s. at all times). (War Memorial and Precincts free.) *Official Guide Book.* 2s. 3d. *Popular Guide Book.* 1s. 6d. *Folder Guide* (English and French). 4d. *Folder Guide to Scottish United Services Museum.* 4d. *Telephone No.:* 031–229 2585 (Weekends, 031–225 5892).

Edinburgh: Corstorphine Dovecot

A fine dovecot in a good state of preservation, with nesting boxes within; circular in plan; dates from the seventeenth century.
Situation. In the suburb of Corstorphine (Dovecot Road), Edinburgh. O.S. 1″ map sheet 62, ref. NT 200725.
Admission. All times without charge. For key Telephone 031–229 2585 or from Edinburgh Tapestry Co., The Dovecot, Dovecot Road, Edinburgh 12.

*Edinburgh: Craigmillar Castle (Plate 21)

This renowned castle, whose fame and form are familar to Scotsmen all the world over, is forever associated with some of the darkest and most tragic episodes in the career of Queen Mary. Its great central fourteenth century tower, built by the Prestons, was enclosed in the early part of the next century by an embattled curtain wall, and within this are stately ranges of apartments dating from the sixteenth and seventeenth centuries. The castle was burned by Hereford in 1544. Within its walls, in 1567, and while the Queen herself was in residence, the "Craigmillar band", as the plot to murder Darnley was called, was signed by some of her nobles. The outbuildings of the castle include an interesting chapel.
Situation. 2½ miles south-east of central Edinburgh, to the east of the Edinburgh–Dalkeith road (A 68). O.S. 1″ map sheet 62, ref. NT 285710.
Hours of Admission. Standard.

F

Admission Fee. 1s.
Official Guide Book. 1s. 3d.

★Edinburgh: Holyrood Abbey and Palace of Holyroodhouse

The Abbey of Holyrood was founded by David I for Augustinian Canons regular. All that remains of the monastic buildings is the ruined nave of the Abbey church. This had been probably the finest piece of design in the thirteenth century ecclesiastical architecture of Scotland. Foundations of King David's church exist on the site of the later chancel. The oldest part of the Palace, which is built against the monastic nave, is the north-west tower, erected by James IV. The rest of the quadrangular building was reconstructed, in the neo-classical style, by the famous architect, Sir William Bruce, to the order of Charles II. James IV's Tower still retains the rooms for ever associated with the tragic happenings of which the Palace of Holyroodhouse became the scene in Queen Mary's reign.

Situation. At the foot of the Canongate, Edinburgh. O.S. 1″ map sheet 62, ref. NT 269739.

Hours of Admission:
Summer Hours (June–September inclusive):

    Weekdays   9.30 a.m.—6 p.m.
    Sundays   11.00 a.m.—6 p.m.

Hours are slightly shorter at other times of the year. The Palace is closed during Royal and State visits and for the visit of the Lord High Commissioner to the General Assembly of the Church of Scotland which normally takes place in May or June each year. Details may be obtained by telephoning the number below.

Admission Fee. Historical and State Apartments. 2s. in Winter, 3s. in Summer (children 1s. at all times). *Official Guide Book.* 1s. 9d. *Popular Guide Book.* 1s. 6d. *Folder Guide* (English and French). 4d. *Telephone No.:* 031–556 1847.

Edinburgh: St. Triduana's Chapel, Restalrig Collegiate Church

According to legend, St. Triduana in the eighth century plucked out her eyes to confound King Nechtan of the Picts who had professed an importunate love; she thereafter retired to Restalrig, where she was buried. Her shrine became a place of pilgrimage for those who were afflicted with diseases of the eye. From the late fifteenth century the shrine was situated in the lower chamber of the king's chapel built by James III adjacent to Restalrig church. The design, a two-storeyed vaulted hexagon, is unique. The lower chapel of St. Triduana survives intact; it was restored in 1907–8 after use as a burial-vault. The upper chamber, a chapel of unknown dedication, was demolished in 1560.

Situation. In the Restalrig district, on the east side of Edinburgh. O.S. 1″ map sheet 62, ref. NT 284745. *Admission.* Without charge. Standard hours on application to key-keeper, Mrs. W. Askings, 13 Parson's Green Terrace, Edinburgh 7. *Telephone No.:* 031–661 2924.

MORAY

Burghead Well

This remarkable rock-cut structure, within the *murus Gallicus* of an Iron Age fort, is probably an early Christian baptistery, associated with the local *cultus* of St. Ethan. The locality is famous for the number of stones with figures of bulls, incised in the style of the oldest Pictish symbols, that it has yielded.

Situation. At Burghead, 8 miles north-west of Elgin. O.S. 1″ map sheet 29, ref. NJ 110692.

Admission. All times without charge.

Duffus Castle

The original seat of the de Moravia or Murray family, now represented by the ducal houses of Atholl and Sutherland. This is the finest example of a motte and bailey castle in the north of Scotland, and is unique by reason of the wide outer precinct ditch, enclosing eight acres, which surrounds the castle. About 1300 the bailey was walled in, and a great stone tower, of very fine workmanship, was erected on the mount, which has slipped under its weight, splitting the tower in two. Within the curtain are remains of a hall, reconstructed in the fifteenth century.

Situation. At Old Duffus, 3 miles north-west of Elgin. O.S. 1″ map sheet 29, ref. NJ 189673.

Admission. All times without charge.

Official Guide Pamphlet. 6d. (Available at Elgin Cathedral and St. Peter's Church, Duffus).

Duffus: St. Peter's Church and Parish Cross

Duffus Church retains the base of a fourteenth century western tower, a fine vaulted porch of the sixteenth century, and some interesting tombstones. The Parish Cross, a tall and elegant cross shaft apparently of fourteenth century date, about 14 feet high, stands upon its original stepped base. An enriched band circles the shaft near the top: the cross head is much weathered.

Situation. In Duffus churchyard, 4½ miles north-west of Elgin. O.S. 1″ map sheet 29, ref. NJ 175687.

Admission. All times without charge.

*Elgin Cathedral (Plate 16)

When entire, this was perhaps the most beautiful of our Scottish cathedrals. The remains consist of a nave with double aisles and north and south porches; twin western towers having a superb portal and window between; transepts, above which rose a great central tower, now gone; choir with aisles and presbytery; and a detached octagonal chapter-house. The cathedral was founded in 1224, and much of the remaining work is in the style of that century: but in 1390 the church was burned by the "Wolf of Badenoch", and the ruins thus show traces of extensive reconstruction subsequent to this catastrophe. The early work betrays strong French influence. The chapter-house, reconstructed in the fifteenth century, is the finest of its kind in Scotland. In the surviving ruins, and in the detached fragments assembled on the site, there is a wealth of moulded work, heraldic decoration, and figure sculpture, forming a notable conspectus of the medieval mason-craftsman's art. Preserved in the nave is a fine Celtic cross-slab, with Pictish symbols.

Situation. In Elgin. O.S. 1″ map sheet 29, ref. NJ 223630.

Hours of Admission. Standard.

Admission Fee. 1s.

Official Guide Book. 1s. 9d.

Elgin: "Bishop's House"

A small remnant of what is by tradition the town house of the Bishops of Moray immediately opposite Elgin Cathedral. It now forms a picturesque ruin, and possesses some pleasing architectural features, notably a fine oriel window. The crow steps of the gables are themselves gabled. Coats of arms on the building include those of Bishop Patrick Hepburn (1535–73) and Robert Reid, Abbot of Kinloss and Bishop of Orkney (1541–58). The oldest stone is dated 1557.

Situation. North-west of Elgin Cathedral. O.S. 1″ map sheet 29, ref. NJ 222631.

Admission. Not yet open to the public.

Sueno's Stone (Plate 7)

One of the most remarkable early sculptured monuments in Scotland; 20 feet high. On one side a tall cross accompanied by once elaborate figure sculpture at the base; on the other sculptured groups of figures of warriors, etc., disposed as though depicting hunting and warlike scenes.

Situation. At the east end of Forres, beside the road to Kinloss (B 9011). O.S. 1″ map sheet 29, ref. NJ 047595.

Admission. All times without charge.

NAIRNSHIRE

Ardclach Bell Tower

The tower is 14 feet square and contains two storeys. A straight stone stair leads from the vaulted ground floor to the upper floor. This has a fireplace, on either side of which is a square gun-loop with well-splayed openings towards the interior, and a square aperture to the exterior. The side gable is also equipped with a small gun-loop. The apex of this gable is surmounted by a small belfry wherein was housed the bell which summoned the worshippers to the Parish Church of Ardclach nearby, and doubtless, also, as may be inferred from the prominent position of this little structure, gave warning to the neighbourhood in cases of alarm. The tower is dated 1655.

Situation. 8½ miles south-east of Nairn, west of the road to Grantown-on-Spey (A 939). O.S. 1″ map sheet 29, ref. NH 954453.

Admission. All reasonable times, on application to custodian.

ORKNEY

NOTE:

Monuments on the mainland are easily accessible. The Brough of Birsay site is on a tidal island. There is no crossing by boat. Crossing by foot is impossible in the period approximately 3 hours before High Water to 3 hours after it. High Water is an hour before High Water at Kirkwall, which is intimated at the Harbourmaster's office there. Visitors can enquire about access by telephoning the custodian, Mr. Matches, Birsay 272.

There is a daily boat to Rousay from Mainland by Mr. Magnus Flaws, Tel. Wyre 203, who can arrange for motor-boat transport to Rousay, Egilsay, Eynhallow and Wyre at other times as well. Intending visitors to Rousay should contact the key-keeper of the monuments, Mr. Marwick, Tel. Wasbister 4, for motor transport on that island, which has no 'bus service.

A regular steamer operates from Kirkwall and visitors to Sanday, Westray, and Holm of Papa Westray should consult the timetable. Hoy is reached by boat from Stromness, operated by Mr. Angus Brown, Tel. Stromness 240, and a car can be hired on the island by arrangement with Mr. Moar, Tel. Hoy 201. The custodian of the Holm of Papa Westray Cairn is Mr. Rendall, Cuppins, Papa Westray, whose boat will be required for the short crossing to the Holm. There is also a daily inter-island air service. For further information visitors should consult Mr. Windwick, custodian at the Earl's Palace, Kirkwall.

The attention of visitors is drawn to the Official Guide Book to Orkney monuments, obtainable from the Stationery Office and at the principal monuments on the Orkney Mainland. Price 2s. 9d.

MAINLAND

Birsay, Earl's Palace

Extensive but dilapidated ruin of palace built for Robert Earl of Orkney in 1574. The buildings occupy four sides of a courtyard, with projecting rectangular towers at three of the four corners. Few details of the interior arrangements can now be identified.

Situation. Near the shore, 1 mile south-east of the Brough of Birsay at the end of road A 966. O.S. 1″ map sheet 6, ref. HY 246280.

Admission. At all times without charge.

Birsay, The Brough of

On this tidal island stands a ruined Romansesque church, consisting of nave chancel and semicircular apse, with claustral buildings appended on the north side. No record of the monastery has survived. A magnificent sculptured stone, with Pictish symbols and three warriors in procession, was discovered in the ruins and is now in the National Museum. Close beside the church, remains of Viking dwellings have been unearthed and are now conserved.

Situation. At Birsay, north end of Mainland, 20 miles north-west of Kirkwall. O.S. 1″ map sheet 6, HY 239285.

Admission. All reasonable times but closed on Mondays in winter. Crossings by foot except at High Water. No crossings by boat.

Admission Fee. 1s.

Official Guide Book. The Early Christian and Norse Settlements, Birsay. Price 1s. 6d. (Available at major monuments in Orkney.)

Cuween Hill Cairn

A low mound covering a megalithic passage tomb. The main chamber contains four mural cells. Contained the bones of men, dogs and oxen when discovered. Probably early second millennium B.C.

Situation. About ½ mile south of Finstown which is 6 miles west-north-west of Kirkwall (route A 965). O.S. 1″ map sheet 6, ref. HY 364128.

Admission. All reasonable times without charge, on application to key-keeper at nearby farmhouse.

Dounby Click Mill

The only working example of the old Orcadian horizontal water-mills.

Situation. 2 miles north-west of Dounby, on route B 9057. O.S. 1″ map sheet 6, ref. HY 325228.

Admission. All times without charge.

Official Guide Pamphlet. 3d. (Available at Earl's Palace, Kirkwall.)

Grain Earth-house

A well-built Iron Age souterrain or earth-house comprising entrance stair, passage and underground chamber; the roof is supported by stone pillars.

Situation. About ¾ mile north-west of Kirkwall within the boundaries of the old Hatston airfield. O.S. 1″ map sheet 6, ref. HY 442117.

Admission. All reasonable times without charge, on application to key-keeper, Miss H. E. Johnstone, 37 Hatston Houses, Kirkwall.

(The Broch of)
*Gurness, Aikerness

An Iron Age broch tower still standing over 10 feet high surrounded by a complex of secondary huts and other buildings, the whole encircled by a deep rock-cut ditch. The site was later inhabited in Dark Age and Viking times.

Situation. On the coast at Aikerness, near Evie, about 11 miles north-west of Kirkwall and 1½ miles north of the main road (A 966). O.S. 1″ map sheet 6, ref. HY 383268.

Hours of Admission. Standard, but closed on Saturdays during winter.
Admission Fee. 1s.
Official Guide Pamphlet. 6d.

*Kirkwall: The Bishop's Palace

An extensive ruin closely adjoining the Cathedral. The main portion consists of a hall-house dating originally from the twelfth century, but much altered subsequently, in particular by Bishop Reid (1541–8) who added a powerful round tower, embattled and pierced for guns. A still later addition was made by Patrick Stewart, Earl of Orkney, about 1600.

Situation. In Kirkwall, south of the cathedral. O.S. 1″ map sheet 6, ref. HY 447108.

Admission. See under Earl Patrick's Palace.

*Kirkwall: Earl Patrick's Palace

This magnificent building, which stands, roofless, but otherwise almost complete, immediately opposite the Bishop's Palace, has been well described as "the most mature and accomplished piece of Renaissance architecture left in Scotland". It forms three sides of a square, and is distinguished by the ability of its planning and the masterly refinement of its architectural details. Notable features are the great oriel windows, in the French manner. The palace was built by Earl Patrick Stewart between 1600 and 1607, but the full design was never completed.

Situation. In Kirkwall, south of the cathedral. O.S. 1″ map sheet, 6 ref. HY 448108.

Admission Fee. 1s. (Including Bishop's Palace).

	Weekdays	Sundays
April–September ..	9.30 a.m.—7 p.m.	2 p.m.—7 p.m.
October–March ..	10 a.m.—Dusk	2 p.m.—Dusk

Official Guide Book. 1s. 6d.

*Maes Howe

The finest megalithic tomb in the British Isles, the masonry being unsurpassed in Western Europe. A large mound covers a stone-built passage and large corbelled burial chamber with mural cells; *c.* 1800 B.C.; plundered in Viking times. Norse runes are inscribed on several stones.

Situation. About 9 miles west of Kirkwall, on the main Stromness road (A 965). O.S. 1″ map sheet 6, ref. HY 318128.

Admission:		*Weekdays*	*Sundays*
April—September	..	All reasonable	2 p.m.—7 p.m.
October—March	..	times.	2 p.m.—4 p.m.

Apply to key-keeper in nearby farmhouse.

Admission Fee. 1s.

Official Guide Pamphlet. 1s.

*Unstan or Onston, Cairn

An almost circular mound bounded by three concentric walls and covering a megalithic burial chamber divided by upright slabs into five compartments; of late third millennium B.C. date. Fragments of over 22 pottery bowls of a type now known as the Unstan class of Neolithic pottery were found in the chamber.

Situation. About 2½ miles north-east of Stromness on the Kirkwall road (A 965). O.S. 1″ map sheet 6, ref. HY 283117.

Admission. All reasonable times without charge, on application to key-keeper.

Orphir Church and Earl's Bu

Only the chancel and a small part of the nave remain of this, the single example of a round church known to have been built in the Middle Ages in Scotland. The structure dates from the twelfth century, and appears to have been modelled on Scandinavian prototypes, derived ultimately from the Church of the Holy Sepulchre at Jerusalem. Adjacent are the partly excavated foundations of ancient buildings which may be an Earl's palace of Viking times mentioned in the *Orkneyinga Saga.*

Situation. 8 miles west-south-west of Kirkwall on the north shore of Scapa Flow (route A 964). O.S. 1″ map sheet 6, ref. HY 334043.

Admission. All times without charge.

Rennibister Earth-house

An excellent example of the Orkney type of Iron Age souterrain or earth-house consisting of a passage and underground chamber with supporting roof-pillars.

Situation. About 4½ miles west-north-west of Kirkwall on the Finstown road (A 965). O.S. 1″ map sheet 6, ref. HY 397127.

Admission. All reasonable times without charge, on application to key-keeper in farmhouse.

Ring of Brogar (Plate 2)

A magnificent circle of upright stones with enclosing ditch spanned by causeway; *c.* 1600 B.C.

Situation. Between Loch of Harray and Loch of Stenness on road B 9055, about 4 miles north-east of Stromness. O.S. 1″ map sheet 6, ref. HY 294134.
Admission. All times without charge.

Stones of Stenness

The remains of a stone circle standing on a mound of platform encircled by a ditch and bank; second millennium B.C.
Situation. On the southern shore of Loch of Harray on route B 9055, about 4 miles north-east of Stromness. O.S. 1″ map sheet 6, ref. HY 306126.
Admission. All times without charge.

Skara Brae: Prehistoric Village (Plate 1)

An impressive cluster of dwellings preserved in drift sand. The dwellings—rectangular rooms with rounded corners—and passages are amazingly conserved with their stone furniture, hearths and drains (*c.* 1600–1400 B.C.).
Situation. Bay of Skaill, on the west coast about 6 miles north-north-west of Stromness (B 9056). O.S. 1″ map sheet 6, ref. HY 231188.
From Kirkwall, 19 miles north-west, and from Stromness 7 miles to the north.
Hours of Admission. Standard.
Admission Fee. 1s.
Official Guide Book. 1s. 9d.

Wideford Hill Cairn

A conspicuous megalithic chambered cairn with three concentric walls. The burial chamber with three large cells leading off it is entered by passage; of early second millennium B.C. date.
Situation. 2½ miles west of Kirkwall on the west slope of Wideford Hill. O.S. 1″ map sheet 6, ref. HY 409122.
Admission. All reasonable times without charge, on application to the key-keeper.

ISLAND OF EGILSAY
St. Magnus Church

This remarkable structure, roofless but otherwise almost entire, consists of a nave, a square-ended and vaulted chancel, and a western tower, the latter being tall and cylindrical, somewhat after the manner of the Celtic round towers such as those at Brechin and Abernethy. Above the chancel vault there was a room. A church existed here in 1116, when St. Magnus was martyred either in the building or just outside it. It seems probable, however, that the existing structure dates from nearer the end of that century.
Situation. On the island of Egilsay. O.S. 1″ map sheet 6, ref. HY 466304.
Admission. All reasonable times without charge, key from nearby farmhouse.

ISLAND OF EYNHALLOW
Eynhallow Church

A twelfth century church, consisting of nave, chancel and west porch, all greatly altered and now much ruined. Close by is a group of domestic buildings, likewise much ruined. A monastery is known to have existed on the

island, but it is doubtful whether any of its remains can be recognized in the surviving ruins.
Situation. On the island of Eynhallow. O.S. 1″ map sheet 6, ref. HY 359289.
Admission. All times without charge.

ISLAND OF HOY

Dwarfie Stane

A huge block of sandstone in which a burial chamber has been quarried resembling the rock-cut chambered tombs common in the Mediterranean, Portugal, and other parts of the Atlantic megalithic province. No other tomb of this type is known in the British Isles. Probably *c.* 2000–1600 B.C.
Situation. On the island of Hoy. O.S. 1″ map sheet 6, ref. HY 244005.
Admission. All times without charge. Access by boat from Stromness.

ISLAND OF ROUSAY

Blackhammer Cairn

A long cairn bounded by a well-preserved retaining wall and containing a megalithic burial chamber divided into seven compartments or stalls; probably second millennium B.C.
Situation. On the south coast of the island, north of B 9064. O.S. 1″ map sheet 6, ref. HY 414276.
Admission. All reasonable times without charge.

Knowe of Yarso Cairn

An oval cairn with concentric casing walls enclosing a megalithic chambered tomb divided by paired upright slabs into three compartments or stalls; probably second millennium B.C.
Situation. On the south coast of the island, north of B 9064. O.S. 1″ map sheet 6, ref. HY 403281.
Admission. All reasonable times without charge.

Midhowe Broch

An Iron Age broch tower and walled enclosure situated on a promontory cut off by a deep rock-cut ditch. The court-like enclosure contains secondary buildings.
Situation. On the west coast of the island. O.S. 1″ sheet map 6, ref. HY 371308.
Admission. All reasonable times without charge.

Midhowe Cairn (Plate 3)

An impressive megalithic chambered tomb contained in an oval barrow with three concentric casing walls. The chamber is divided into 12 compartments containing stone slab benches; probably second millennium B.C.
Situation. On the west coast of the island, close to Midhowe Broch. O.S. 1″ map sheet 6, ref. NY 372306.
Admission. All reasonable times without charge.

Taversöe Tuick Cairn

A megalithic chambered burial mound containing two burial chambers divided into stalls; *c.* 2000 B.C.

Situation. On the south coast of the island north of road B 9064. O.S. 1″ map sheet 6, ref. HY 426276.
Admission. All reasonable times without charge.

ISLAND OF SANDAY

Quoyness Cairn

A megalithic chambered cairn with triple retaining walls containing a passage and main chamber with six beehive cells; probably second millennium B.C.
Situation. At Quoy Ness on the south coast of the island. O.S. 1″ map sheet 5, ref. HY 677378.
Admission. All reasonable times without charge, on application to key-keeper, Mr. W. S. Muir, Bridgend, Sanday, Orkney. Island steamer service from Kirkwall.

ISLAND OF WESTRAY

*Noltland Castle

A fine ruin on the Z-plan, with square towers at each of two diagonally opposite corners. This castle is remarkable for its tiers of yawning gun-loops, giving it the external semblance of some ancient man-o'-war's hull. It was built by Gilbert Balfour of Westray, between 1560 and 1573, but never completed. Here some of Montrose's officers found refuge after his last defeat in 1650.
Situation. ½ mile west-north-west of Pierowall. O.S. 1″ map sheet 5, ref. HY 429488.
Admission. All reasonable times without charge, on application to custodian.
Official Guide Pamphlet. 6d.

Pierowall Church

A ruin consisting of nave and chancel, the latter canted. There are some finely lettered tombstones.
Situation. At Pierowall. O.S. 1″ map sheet 5, ref. HY 438487.
Admission. All times without charge.

Westside (Tuquoy Church)

A twelfth century church, with nave and chancel, the former lengthened in the later Middle Ages. The chancel has a Romanesque arch and was vaulted.
Situation. Bay of Tuquoy, on the south coast of the island. O.S. 1″ map sheet 5, ref. HY 455432.
Admission. All times without charge.

ISLAND OF PAPA WESTRAY

Knap of Howar

The ruins of two stone structures lying side by side, apparently of a domestic character, recently uncovered by excavation. The character of the masonry suggests parallels with the secondary buildings at the Broch of Gurness.
Situation. West side of island of Papa Westray, near Holland House. O.S. 1″ map sheet 5, ref. HY 483519.
Admission. All times without charge.

HOLM OF PAPA WESTRAY
Cairn

A megalithic chambered cairn of Neolithic date (c. 1800 B.C.). The long narrow chamber is divided into three sub-divisions by transverse walls, while 14 beehive cells open off the walls. Engravings occur—rare examples of megalithic art in Scotland.

Situation. On the east side of the island. O.S. 1″ map sheet 5, ref. HY 509518.
Admission. All reasonable times without charge, on application to custodian, Mr. Rendall, Holland, Papa Westray.

ISLAND OF WYRE
Cobbie Row's Castle

This remote structure is probably the earliest stone castle authenticated in Scotland. The *Orkneyinga Saga* tells how about 1145 Kolbein Hruga built a fine stone castle (*steinkastala*) in Wyre. His name, in a corrupted form, is still attached to the present ruins, and as careful excavation has failed to yield traces of any earlier structure, there can be little doubt that the existing remains represent the *steinkastala*. It consists of a small rectangular tower, enclosed in a circular ditch, and associated with later buildings.

Situation. In the centre of the island. O.S. 1″ map sheet 6, ref. HY 442264.
Admission. All times without charge.

St. Mary's Chapel

In a graveyard near the middle of the island of Wyre is a ruinous chapel of the late twelfth century said to have been dedicated to St. Mary although commonly attributed to St. Peter. It is a small rectangular Romanesque structure of nave and chancel. The walls are built of local whinstone. The entrance is in the centre of the west gable through a semi-circular archway. The entrance to the chancel is similar.

Situation. Near Cobbie Row's Castle. O.S. 1″ map sheet 6, ref. HY 443264.
Admission. All times without charge.

PEEBLESSIIIRE

Peebles: Cross Kirk

The remains of a Trinitarian Friary, consisting of the nave and west tower. The foundations of the claustral building, which were on the north side of the nave, have been laid bare.

Situation. In Peebles. O.S. 1″ map sheet 62, ref. NT 250408.
Hours of Admission. Standard. Without charge. Key from custodian in nearby house.

PERTHSHIRE

Abernethy Round Tower

One of the two remaining Irish round towers in Scotland (see also BRECHIN, ANGUS). It dates from about the end of the eleventh century, and the belfry windows are of Romanesque character. Beside it is preserved a Pictish symbol stone.

Situation. In Abernethy. O.S. 1″ map sheet 55, ref. NO 191165.
Admission. All reasonable times without charge on application to custodian.

*Dunblane Cathedral

One of Scotland's noblest medieval churches. The existing building dates mainly from the thirteenth century, but embodies a square tower, once free-standing, the lower part of which is Norman work. The cathedral consists of an aisled nave, an aisleless choir, and a lady-chapel attached to the north wall of the choir. There are no transepts. The nave was unroofed after the Reformation, but the whole building was restored in 1892–5. Apart from the Norman tower, the oldest portion is the Lady chapel. The church contains some good monuments, also important remnants of the medieval carved oaken stalls. In the nave are buried James IV's mistress, Margaret Drummond, and her two sisters, all poisoned at Drummond Castle in 1502.

Situation. In Dunblane. O.S. 1″ map sheet 54, ref. NN 782015.

Admission. Standard (except Sundays in Summer when 2 p.m. to 5.30 p.m.). Without charge.

Telephone No.: 0786 82 2321.

Dunfallandy Stone

An eighth century Pictish cross-slab with a cross, beasts and angels on one side, and with a horseman, seated figures, and Pictish symbols on the other. The stone originally stood near Killiecrankie.

Situation. South of Dunfallandy House, 1½ miles south-south-east of Pitlochry. O.S. 1″ map sheet 49, ref. NN 946565.

Admission. All times without charge.

*Dunkeld Cathedral

Beautifully situated on the north bank of the Tay, this is the most romantic of the Scottish cathedrals. The choir has been restored and is in use as the parish church. The nave and the great north-west tower date from the fifteenth century, and are in the custody of the Ministry of Public Building and Works. There are interesting early sixteenth century wall paintings in the aisle under the Tower. The choir contains the monument of the "Wolf of Badenoch", and the chapter-house is now the mausoleum of the Dukes of Atholl.

Situation. In Dunkeld. O.S. 1″ map sheet 49, ref. NO 025426.

Hours of Admission. Standard.

Admission Fee. 1s.

Official Guide Book. 1s. 6d.

*Elcho Castle

This very fine and picturesque example of a sixteenth century fortified mansion survives intact, and is remarkable for its great development of tower-like "jambs" or wings, and for the wrought iron grilles which protect its windows. It is well equipped for firearms and is strongly situated on the edge of the quarry from which it was built. The castle is an ancestral seat of the Earls of Wemyss.

Situation. On the south bank of the Tay, 3½ miles south-east of Perth. O.S. 1″ map sheet 55, ref. NO 164211.

Hours of Admission. Standard.

Admission Fee. 1s.

Telephone No.: 0738 23437.

Fowlis Wester: Sculptured Stone

A fine cross-slab, 10 feet high, with Pictish symbols, figure and animal sculpture, and Celtic enrichment. The cross is unique in that its arms extend beyond the slab.

Situation. At Fowlis Wester, 4 miles east-north-east of Crieff to the north of the Perth road (A 85). O.S. 1 map sheet 55, ref. NN 928241.

Admission. Can be viewed closely from the churchyard.

Grandtully: St. Mary's Church

A sixteenth century church, close to Grandtully Castle, remarkable for its finely painted wooden ceiling, with heraldic and symbolic subjects.

Situation. At Pitcairn Farm, 2 miles east-north-east of Aberfeldy. O.S. 1″ map sheet 48, ref. NN 886506.

Admission. All times without charge, on application to custodian.

*Huntingtower, or Ruthven Castle

A very castellated mansion of the fifteenth and sixteenth centuries beautifully situated on a steep bank overlooking the Almond. It is remarkable by reason of its well-preserved painted ceiling. The ancient seat of the Ruthvens, Earls of Gowrie, it became famous in 1582 as the scene of the "Raid of Ruthven" when the young King James VI was kidnapped by the Earls of Mar and Gowrie.

Situation. 2 miles west of Perth on the Perth–Crieff road (A 85). O.S. 1″ map sheet 55, ref. NO 084252.

Hours of Admission. Standard.

Admission Fee. 1s.

Official Guide Book. 1s. 3d.

*Inchmahome Priory

This beautifully situated monastic house, on an island in the Lake of Menteith, is famous as the retreat of the infant Mary Queen of Scots. It was an Augustinian house, founded by Walter Comyn, Earl of Menteith, in 1238. Considerable parts of the church and claustral buildings remain, including much fine work of the thirteenth century. The recumbent monuments of Walter, first Stewart Earl of Menteith and his Countess still survive, as well as that of Sir John Drummond, a fifteenth century benefactor. Remains of the monastic gardens are still traceable.

Situation. On an island in the Lake of Menteith 3 miles east of Aberfoyle. O.S. 1″ map sheet 54, ref. NN 574005.

Access. By ferry from Port of Menteith on request.

Hours of Admission. April to Mid-November, Standard (Weather conditions permitting). From Mid-November to 31st March, ferry service has normally to be suspended. Telephone enquiries to 0786 3360.

Admission Fee. 1s. Ferry to the island, 1s.

Official Guide Pamphlet. 6d.

Innerpeffray Church

The church stands on a high knoll overlooking the River Earn, near the ruined castle of Innerpeffray and the well-known library founded by Lord Madderty in 1691. The church was built in 1508 by Sir John Drummond of

Innerpeffray as a collegiate foundation dedicated to the Blessed Virgin. It is a small, plain, long narrow building, still entire, containing such features of interest as an original altar stone, corbels to support a rood loft and part of a small tempera-painted ceiling.

Situation. 3 miles south-east of Crieff, on a turning off the Auchterarder road (B 8062). O.S. 1″ map sheet 55, ref. NN 902185.

Admission. At all reasonable times without charge. Closed on Thursdays.

★*Meigle: Sculptured Stones* (Plate 6)

Housed in a museum here, is a magnificent collection of 25 sculptured monuments of the Celtic Christian period, all found at or near the old churchyard. Many of these monuments are of the highest artistic and symbolic interest, and the whole collection forms one of the most notable assemblages of Dark Age sculpture in Western Europe.

Situation. At Meigle, on the Coupar Angus–Forfar road (A 94). O.S. 1″ map sheet 49, ref. NN 287446.

Hours of Admission. Standard; but closed on Sundays.

Admission Fee. 1s.

Official Guide Pamphlet. 3d. The Guide Book of Early Christian and Pictish Monuments is also available, 5s.

Muthill Old Church and Tower

The very interesting ruins of an important medieval parish church, about three miles south of Crieff. At its west end, embedded in the nave, is a tall Norman tower, with good architectural detail. It was once free-standing, like the tower at Dunblane Cathedral. The nave and chancel belong mostly to the early fifteenth century, but the sedilia and some other details are of First Pointed character. There was a Culdee settlement here, and the tall free-standing tower partakes somewhat of a Celtic character.

Situation. At Muthill, 3 miles south of Crieff on the Dunblane road (A 822). O.S. 1″ map sheet 55, ref. NN 868171.

Admission. All times without charge.

Tullibardine Chapel

This is one of the few Collegiate Churches in Scotland which was entirely finished and still remains unaltered. It was founded by Sir David Murray of Dumbarton, ancestor of the Duke of Atholl, in 1446. It is cruciform in plan and has a small western tower entering from the church by a narrow doorway. Each part of the church is of equal size. There is good moulded detail round the internal and external openings. The gable ends are finished with the typical Scottish crow-step of the domestic tradition.

Situation. 6 miles south-east of Crieff off the main Auchterarder road (A 823). O.S. 1″ map sheet 55, ref. NN 909135.

Admission. All reasonable times without charge, on application to the key-holder, Mr. Maxtone, at adjacent farmhouse.

RENFREWSHIRE

Barochan Cross, Houston

A fine, free-standing Celtic cross, 11 feet high, with figure sculpture. Not on its original site.

Situation. 1¼ miles north of Houston which is 5 miles north-west of the centre of Paisley. O.S. 1″ map sheet 60, ref. NS 406690.
Admission. All times without charge.

Castle Semple Collegiate Church

The church is a rectangular structure with an apsidal east end. A square tower projects from the west gable. The style of the east end is remarkable. The apse is three-sided, each side having three windows of debased Gothic form. An ornate monument in memory of John Lord Semple, killed at Flodden, 1513, is in the north wall at the east end. It reveals the last expiring effort of the Gothic decorative spirit.
Situation. At Castle Semple, 1½ miles north-east of Lochwinnoch. O.S. 1″ map sheet 60, ref. NS 376601.
Admission. Not yet open to the public. May be viewed from the outside.

*Newark Castle

A large and fine turreted mansion of the Maxwells, still almost entire. It dates mostly from the sixteenth and seventeenth centuries, but embodies an earlier tower-house. The mansion forms three sides of a square.
Situation. In a shipyard in Port Glasgow. O.S. 1″ map sheet 60, ref. NS 329744.
Hours of Admission. Standard, but notice posted when keyholder absent.
Admission Fee. 1s.

ROSS AND CROMARTY

"Black House"

No. 42, Arnol, Lewis

A good example of a traditional type of Hebridean dwelling, built without mortar and roofed with thatch on a timber framework and without eaves. Characteristic features are the central peat fire in the kitchen, the absence of any chimney, and the byre under the same roof. The house retains many of its original furnishings, including the box beds and dresser, and was occupied until the 1950s.
Situation. At Arnol, 15 miles north-west of Stornoway, on the A 858. O.S. 1″ map sheet 8, NB 311488.
Admission. Weekdays, April to September 12 noon–2 p.m. and 5 p.m.–7 p.m.
                        October to March 12 noon–2 p.m.
                        Closed on Sundays.
Admission Fee. 1s.

Callanish Standing Stones, Lewis

A cruciform setting of megaliths unique in Scotland and outstanding in Great Britain. The complex comprises an avenue, 27 feet wide, of nineteen standing stones, and 270 feet long terminating in a circle 37 feet in diameter, of thirteen standing stones from which extend on either side a cross row of four stones and beyond a shorter avenue, 12 feet wide of six stones. Associated are two cairns, one lying within the circle and one touching it. The scheme was probably not a single conception but carried out in a series of additions. Other groups of stone circles are in the near vicinity. Probably *c.* 2000–1500 B.C.

Situation. On the ridge of a promontory extending into Loch Roag about 13 miles west of Stornoway off the A 858. O.S. 1″ map sheet 8, ref. NB 213331.
Admission. All times without charge.

Dun Carloway Broch, Lewis

One of the best preserved Iron Age broch towers in the Western Isles. Still standing about 30 feet high.
Situation. 1½ miles south-west of Carloway and about 15 miles west-north-west of Stornoway off the A 858. O.S. 1″ map sheet 8, ref. NB 190413.
Admission. All times without charge.

Fortrose Cathedral and Precincts

The existing portions of the cathedral are the south aisle of the nave and the nearby sacristy or undercroft of the chapter-house. Such portions of the cathedral as exist are complete, including the vaulting overhead, and there is much fine detail to be seen of fourteenth century date. The undercroft of the chapter-house is probably earlier; mid-thirteenth century.
Situation. In Fortrose. O.S. 1″ map sheet 28, ref. NH 728565.
Admission. All reasonable times without charge, on application to custodian.

"Steinacleit" Cairn and Stone Circle, Lewis

The fragmentary remains of a chambered cairn of Neolithic date (*c.* 2000 B.C.).
Situation. At the south end of Loch an Duin, Shader, 12 miles north of Stornoway, off the A 857. O.S. 1″ map sheet 8, ref. NB 396541.
Admission. All times without charge.

ROXBURGHSHIRE

*Hermitage Castle (Plate 19)

This vast ruin, standing amid lonely and barren hills, was the ancient stronghold of the de Soulis family, and later of the Douglases. Its history is associated with many stirring and some cruel incidents. The castle has been much added to and altered at various times, and was extensively restored in the early nineteenth century, so that its architectural history is obscure: but the oldest work seems to date from the fourteenth century. Here, in October 1566, Queen Mary visited her wounded lover, Bothwell.
Situation. In Liddesdale, 5½ miles north-east of Newcastleton. O.S. 1″ map sheet 69, ref. NY 497961.
Hours of Admission. Standard.
Admission Fee. 1s.
Official Guide Book. 1s. 3d.

*Jedburgh Abbey

A house of Augustinian canons regular, and one of the four famous Border monasteries founded by David I. The remains of the church are mostly Norman or Transitional, and present some remarkable features, notably in the arcading of the choir, an obvious reminiscence of the underslung triforium of Oxford Cathedral. Jedburgh possesses the only complete, or nearly complete, Transitional west front in Scotland. Interesting remnants of the claustra buildings have been uncovered. There is a small museum, including many carved fragments of medieval work and some important monuments of the Anglian period.

Situation. In Jedburgh (route A 68). O.S. 1″ map sheet 70, ref. NT 650205.

Hours of Admission. Standard.

Admission Fee. 1s.

Card Guide. 2d. The Scottish Border Abbeys Popular Guide is also available, price 2s.

*Kelso Abbey

Another of David I's great foundations, this time for monks of the Tironensian Order. Little but the abbey church remains, and that only in imposing fragments: but the building, which is almost wholly of Norman and Transitional work is unique in Scotland because the plan has had western as well as eastern transepts, with a tower over both the crossings. This is the plan of Ely and Bury St. Edmunds, and is derived from the Carolingian and Ottonian minsters of the Rhineland. The best preserved portion is the north transept, a superb piece of design.

Situation. In Kelso. O.S. 1″ map sheet 70, ref. NT 729338.

Hours of Admission. Standard, without charge, but notice posted when keyholder absent.

Guide Book. Scottish Border Abbeys Popular Guide, 2s.

*Melrose Abbey (Plate 12)

Probably the most famous ruin in Scotland, this beautiful Cistercian abbey, founded by David I, was repeatedly wrecked in the Wars of Independence, notably by Richard II, in 1385. Most of the surviving remains belong to the fifteenth century reconstruction, and represent the finest flowering of Scottish Decorated work. Much of the tracery is obviously derived from York, and probably was designed to fit glass imported thence. The beauty of the figure sculpture associated with the church is unrivalled in Scotland. Much progress has been made in laying bare the foundations of the claustral buildings, which were on the north side of the nave. The Commendator's House, an interesting structure, has been fitted up to form a museum. Melrose Abbey owes much of its modern fame to the glamour that has been shed around it by Sir Walter Scott. Somewhere in the church lies buried the heart of Bruce.

Situation. In Melrose (A 6091). O.S. 1″ map sheet 70, ref. NT 549342.

Hours of Admission. Standard.

Admission Fee. 1s.

Official Guide. 2s. *Card Guide.* 4d. Scottish Border Abbeys Popular Guide also available, price 2s.

Telephone No.: 0896 82 262.

Smailholm Tower

The tower has an elevated situation on a rocky outcrop commanding a magnificent panoramic view of the Border country. The tower is a simple rectangle, 57 feet high, in a good state of preservation. It was probably erected in the fifteenth century. The upper part may have been added in the sixteenth century.

Situation. Near the farm of Sandyknowe, 6 miles west of Kelso and 1½ miles south-west of Smailholm. O.S. 1″ map sheet 70, ref. NT 638347.
Admission. All reasonable times without charge on application to key-keeper, at Sandyknowe farmhouse.

SHETLAND

Clickhimin

First occupied in the late Bronze Age (700–500 B.C.), this site was fortified at the beginning of the Iron Age (500–300 B.C.) with a stone built fort with associated internal timber ranges, and a "blockhouse" similar in construction to that at the Ness of Burgi. (See p. 99.) At a later date a broch (which still stands to a height of over 17 feet) was constructed inside the fort. Occupation of the site continued into the later Iron Age "wheel-house" period (2nd to 7th or 8th centuries A.D.).
Situation. About ¾ mile south-west of Lerwick. O.S. map 1″ sheet 4, ref. HU 464408.
Admission. All reasonable times without charge.

Fort Charlotte

A fort roughly pentagonal in shape with bastions projecting from each corner. The walls are high and massive and contain gun ports pointing seawards. It is recorded that the fort was begun in 1665 to protect the Sound of Bressay against the Dutch, and that the architect was John Mylne, the King's master mason. In 1673 it was burned with the town of Lerwick by the Dutch, but in 1781 it was repaired.
Situation. Overlooking the harbour, Lerwick. O.S. 1″ map sheet 4, ref. HU 476418.
Admission. All times without charge.

*Jarlshof (Plate 4)

This is one of the most remarkable archaeological sites in Britain. Within the relatively confined space of three acres are exposed the remains of three extensive village settlements occupied from Bronze Age to Viking times. The first major settlement comprising a collection of oval stone-built huts was excellently preserved by windblown sand. At a higher level the massive walls of an Iron Age broch tower and courtyard protect the most perfect examples known of stone-built wheelhouses still partly roofed and dating to the first centuries of our era. Above the sand which mounded over the structures an entire Viking settlement is preserved, the most complete of its kind yet excavated in the British Isles. The seventeenth century "Laird's House" on the crest of the sandy mound is the original of Sir Walter Scott's "Jarlshof" the home of the fictitious Mr. Mertoun in "The Pirate".
Situation. Sumburgh Head, about 22 miles due south of Lerwick on the southernmost point of Shetland, close to Sumburgh airfield. O.S. 1″ map sheet 4, ref. HU 398096. Bus service from Lerwick to Sumburgh.
Hours of Admission. Standard.
Admission Fee. 1s.
Official Guide Book. 2s. 3d.

Mousa Broch, Mousa (Plate 5)

The best preserved example of the remarkable Iron Age broch towers peculiar to Scotland. The tower still stands to a height of over 40 feet all round and is otherwise complete.

Situation. On the west shore of the island of Mousa, which is off the east coast of the mainland of Shetland. O.S. 1″ map sheet 4, ref. HU 457237. Access by hire of boat from the village of Sandwick about 14 miles south of Lerwick. Daily bus service from Lerwick and Sandwick.

Admission. All times without charge.

Official Guide Book. 1s. (Available at Jarlshof.)

Muness Castle, Unst

Late 16th century building with oblong central block and circular towers at two of the diagonally opposite corners. The castle is characteristically rubble built, but the treatment of shot holes and other architectural detail is exceptionally fine, recalling Scalloway Castle and the Earl's Palace, Kirkwall.

Situation. At the south end of the island of Unst. O.S. 1″ map sheet 1, ref. HP 629013. Access from Lerwick by steamer or overland by bus and ferry.

Admission. All reasonable times without charge on application to key-keeper, Mr. J. Peterson, Castle Cottage, Muness.

Ness of Burgi

A defensive stone-built structure of Iron Age date which is related in certain features to the brochs.

Situation. On the coast at the tip of Scatness about 1 mile south-west of Jarlshof at the south end of the mainland of Shetland. O.S. 1″ map sheet 4, ref. HU 388084.

Admission. All times without charge.

*Scalloway Castle

A fine castellated mansion on the "two-stepped" plan, built in 1600 by the notorious Patrick Stewart, Earl of Orkney (see also under Kirkwall). The memory of the cruelties inflicted upon his tenantry during its erection is preserved in the tale that blood was mixed with the mortar! Earl Patrick paid for his crimes with his life in 1615.

Situation. In Scalloway, about 5 miles west of Lerwick (A 970). O.S. 1″ map sheet 4, ref. HU 405393.

Admission. All reasonable times without charge, on application to custodian.

Official Guide Pamphlet. 6d.

Staneydale

Second millennium B.C. structure, heel-shaped externally, and containing a large oval chamber.

Situation. 2¾ miles east-north-east of Walls. O.S. 1″ map sheet 2, ref. HU 285503.

Admission. All times without charge. Access is through boggy ground.

G*

STIRLINGSHIRE

Antonine Wall and associated works (see p. 35)

Three outstanding lengths of the Antonine Wall, and one wall-fort, are in the custody of the Ministry. These are (from east to west):—

1. *Watling Lodge*. Visible remains of the rampart have been destroyed by agriculture, but the profile of the ditch retains its original V-section.
Situation. 1½ miles west of centre of Falkirk on B 816. O.S. 1″ map sheet 61, ref. NS 862798.

2. *Rough Castle, Roman fort and adjacent length of rampart and ditch*. Rough Catle fort, one of the most notable Roman military sites in Britain, was excsavated by the Society of Antiquaries of Scotland in 1903. It has recently been placed in the custody of the Ministry. A programme of archaeological excavation as a preliminary to consolidation is at present (1969) being carried out. The fort covers about an acre, with double ditches, and an annexe on the east side. Several buildings in the fort, and the bath-house in the annexe, were uncovered in 1903, but their plans cannot now be distinguished on the ground. A unique feature is the series of defensive pits, *lilia*, outside the Antonine ditch on the left front of the fort. Two inscriptions identify the garrison, the 6th Nervian cohort. The site of the fort is a most commanding one, on the brink of a ravine in which descends the Roman Burn.
Situation. 1½ miles east of Bonnybridge. O.S. 1″ map sheet 61, ref. NS 843799.

3. *Seabegs Wood*. A good length of rampart and ditch.
Situation. 1¼ miles south-west of Bonnybridge beside route B 816. O.S. 1″ map sheet 61, ref. NS 814793.
Admission. All times without charge.

★*Cambuskenneth Abbey*

One of the most famous of Scottish monastic houses, and the scene of Bruce's important Parliament in 1326. Here James III and his Queen are buried. The abbey was founded in 1147 by David I as a house of Augustinian Canons regular. The fine detached tower survives complete, but of the church and conventual buildings little save the foundations is now to be seen. The abbey is beautifully situated on the links of the Forth.
Situation. 1 mile east of Stirling. O.S. 1″ map sheet 54, ref. NS 809939.
Admission. Standard but closed in winter.
Admission Fee. 1s.
Official Guide Pamphlet. 6d. (Available at Stirling Castle.)

Stirling: The Argyll Lodging

A great mansion erected about the year 1630; purchased in 1655 by the first Marquess of Argyll. The house has been in use as a military hospital since the later eighteenth century. In scale and architectural character, it is the most impressive town mansion in Scotland of its period. Famous personages associated with it include King Charles II, James VII and the Duke of Cumberland.
Situation. At the top of Castle Wynd, Stirling. O.S. 1″ map sheet 54, ref. NS 793938.
Admission. Not yet open to the public. May be viewed from the outside.

Stirling Castle (cover)

"Stirling, like a huge brooch, clasps Highlands and Lowlands together". Its royal castle on the great basalt rock, 250 feet high, was thus the strategic centre of Scotland, and looks down upon most of the great formative battle fields of Scottish history. As a fortress and a royal palace, its buildings were frequently destroyed and rebuilt, or refashioned at the whim of monarchs. The wonder is that so much of interest survives, including the fine fifteenth century hall, built by James III; the royal palace mostly the work of James V, and showing a quaint mixture of Gothic with Renaissance details; the Chapter Royal, built by James VI for the christening of Prince Henry in 1594; the fine gatehouse of James IV; and important bastioned outworks, dating from the sixteenth, seventeenth and eighteenth centuries. The castle is still in military occupation, so that only parts of it are open to visitors.

Situation. In Stirling. O.S. 1″ map sheet 54, ref. NS 790941.

Hours of Admission:

April—Sept.	..	Weekdays:	10 a.m.—6.45 p.m.
		Sundays:	11 a.m.—6 p.m.
Oct.—March	..	Weekdays:	10 a.m.—4 p.m.
		Sundays:	1 p.m.—4 p.m.

Admission Fee. 1s.
Official Guide Book. 1s. 9d.
Card Guide. 4d.
Telephone No.: 0786 3360.

Stirling: The "King's Knot"

A "knot" garden constructed in the King's Park below the Royal Palace of Stirling. It was one of the earliest ornamental gardens in Scotland and was devised with a layout of lawns and terraces with earthen mounds and ramps.
Situation. Below and to the west of the castle rock by route A 811. Clearly visible from the castle ramparts. O.S. 1″ map sheet 54, ref. NS 789936.
Admission. All times without charge.

Stirling: Mar's Wark

A quaint Renaissance mansion with an ornate gatehouse, enriched with sculptures, heraldic bearings, and humorous rhyming inscriptions. It was built by the Regent Mar in 1570.
Situation. At the top of Castle Wynd, Stirling. O.S. 1″ map sheet 54, ref. NS 793937.
Admission. All times without charge.

Stirling: The Old Bridge

Erected between 1410 and 1415, this fine bridge consists of four arches. The southern one was rebuilt in 1749, after the original arch had been blown up during the Forty-five to prevent the Highlanders entering the town.
Situation. In Stirling, close to route A 9. O.S. 1″ map sheet 54, ref. NS 797946.
Admission. All times without charge.

Westquarter Dovecot

A rectangular type of dovecot of considerable architectural merit. Over the entrance doorway is an heraldic panel dated 1647 containing the arms of Sir

William Livingstone of Westquarter. The shield carries quarterly the arm of Livingstone and Callender. Besides the initials of William Livingstone are those of his wife "D" (for dame) "H." "L."

Situation. In Westquarter, 2¼ miles east-south-east of Falkirk, just north of A 801. O.S. 1″ map sheet 61, ref. NS 913787.

Admission. May be viewed from the outside.

WEST LOTHIAN

*Blackness Castle

At one time one of the most important fortresses in Scotland; used in the seventeenth century as a prison for Covenanters. It comprises a strong, oblong tower, with a circular staircase tower at the north-east angle probably added at a later date. The tower is well-preserved although much altered, and dates from the fifteenth century.

Situation. 4 miles north-east of Linlithgow at end of B 903. O.S. 1″ map sheet 61, ref. NT 055803.

Hours of Admission. Standard.

Admission Fee. 1s.

*Cairnpapple Hill: Sanctuary and Burial Cairns

Originally a sanctuary remodelled in the second millennium B.C. Beaker Period (*c.* 1600 B.C.) as a monumental open air temple in the form of a stone circle with enclosing ditch; later (*c.* 1400 B.C.) despoiled and built over by a Bronze Age cairn, considerably enlarged several centuries later: recently excavated and laid out.

Situation. About 1½ miles east of Torphichen and 3 miles north of Bathgate, O.S. 1″ map sheet 61, ref. NS 987718.

Admission. April–September, Standard. On weekdays in winter by arrangement with custodian at Torphichen Preceptory; Saturdays and Sundays, Standard.

Admission Fee. 1s.

Official Guide Pamphlet. 6d.

Hunter's Craig or Eagle Rock, Cramond

A natural rock with very much defaced carving said to represent an eagle, and to be of Roman date.

Situation. On the foreshore of the Firth of Forth about ¼ mile north-west of Cramond. O.S. 1″ map sheet 62, ref. NT 187775.

Admission. All times without charge.

Kinneil House

The part under guardianship contains important mural and ceiling decorations, of two dates, the earlier executed for the Regent Arran, including the history of the Good Samaritan drawn in the manner of large cartoons for tapestry design: sixteenth and seventeenth centuries.

Situation. 1½ miles west of Bo'ness at south side of Grangemouth road (S 904). O.S. 1″ map sheet 61, ref. NS 983806.

Hours of Admission:	*Weekdays*	*Sundays*
April to September	.. 9.30 a.m. to 7 p.m.	2 p.m. to 7 p.m.
October to March	.. 12 noon to 4 p.m.	2 p.m. to 4 p.m.

Admission Fee. 1s.

Linlithgow Palace (Plate 15)

This ruin, burnt by Hawley's Dragoons in 1746, stands on a mound over-looking Linlithgow Loch. Of Edward 1st's famous Peel nothing now remains, and the oldest part of the existing ruin dates from soon after 1400. The Palace reached its final form in the reign of James V, whose work shows the quaint mixture of Gothic and Renaissance detail characteristic of that reign: the north wing of the Palace was reconstructed in the neo-classical style, between 1618 and 1633. The architecture of all periods is marked by exceptional richness and beauty. Close to the Palace stands the Parish Church of St. Michael, a fine fifteenth century building, still in use, and not under the Ministry's guardianship.

Situation. At Linlithgow on the south shore of the loch. O.S. 1″ map sheet 61, ref. NT 003774.
Hours of Admission. Standard.
Admission Fee. 2s.
Official Guide Book. 2s. 3d.
Telephone No.: 329 2065.

★*Torphichen Preceptory*

This was the principal Scottish seat of the Knights Hospitallers, or Knights of St. John. The central tower and transepts of their church remain, and show the castellated or martial style of ecclesiastical architecture prevalent in Scotland in the fifteenth century. The west tower arch is of Romanesque date: the nave, now the parish church, was rebuilt in the eighteenth century.

Situation. In the village of Torphichen, 2½ miles north of Bathgate (B 792). O.S. 1″ map sheet 61, ref. NS 969725.
Hours of Admission. Standard.
Admission Fee. 1s.
Note: Custodian is also custodian of Cairnpapple Hill.

WIGTOWNSHIRE

Barsalloch Fort

The fort is formed by a deep ditch with a mound on each side; in horseshoe form. The ditch measures 33 feet in width by 12 feet in depth.

Situation. On the hill above the road at Barsalloch Point, ¾ mile west of Monreith (A 747). O.S. 1″ map sheet 80, ref. NX 347412.
Admission. All times without charge.

Big Balcraig and Clachan

Two groups of cup-and-ring engravings of the Bronze Age carved on the natural rock.

Situation. 2¼ miles east of Port William, north of B 7021. O.S. 1″ map sheet 80, ref. NX 374440 and 376445.
Admission. All times without charge.

Chapel Finian

A small chapel or oratory probably of tenth–eleventh century date set within a sub-rectangular enclosure of about 50 feet wide. The chapel is rectangular in plan and only the foundations and lower walls remain. In general appearance the building suggests comparisons with the small early chapels found notably in Ireland.

Situation. 5 miles north-west of Port William on the main Glenluce road (A 747). O.S. 1″ map sheet 79, ref. NX 278489.

Admission. All times without charge.

Druchtag Motehill

The earthwork mound of an early medieval castle, with some traces of stone buildings.

Situation. In Mochrum village, 2 miles north-north-east of Port William, O.S. 1″ map sheet 80, ref. NX 349466.

Admission. All times without charge.

Drumtroddan

A group of cup-and-ring markings of Bronze Age date on a natural rock face, and 400 yards to the south an alignment of three adjacent surviving stones, two upright and one now fallen.

Situation. On Drumtroddan Farm, 1¾ miles north-east of Port William on the Wigtown road (A 714). O.S. 1″ map sheet 80, ref. NX 363447.

Admission. All times without charge.

*Glenluce Abbey

A Cistercian house founded in 1192 by Roland, Earl of Galloway. The ruins occupy a site of great beauty and are in themselves of much architectural distinction and interest. The abbey church is in the First Pointed style, and there is a fine vaulted chapter-house, dating from the later fifteenth century. Of the church, the south aisle and the south transepts are the principal remains. There are some interesting tombstones.

Situation. 2 miles north-west of Glenluce village O S. 1″ map sheet 79, ref. NX 185587.

Hours of Admission. Standard.

Admission Fee. 1s.

Glenluce: Castle of Park

This tall and imposing castellated mansion, still entire, was built, according to an inscription on its walls, by Thomas Hay of Park in 1590. It occupies a conspicuous position on the brow of a hill looking down upon Glenluce. Its builder was a son of the last Abbot of Glenluce.

Situation. ¾ mile west of Glenluce village. O.S. 1″ map sheet 79, ref. NX 189571.

Admission. Not yet open to the public; may be viewed from the outside.

Kirkmadrine: Early Christian Stones

At this lonely church are three of the earliest Christian monuments in Britain, showing the Chi-Rho symbol and inscriptions dating from the fifth or early sixth century.

Situation. In the Rhinns of Galloway 1½ miles south-west of Sandhead and 7½ miles south of Stranraer. O.S. 1″ map sheet 79, ref. NX 081484.

Admission. All times without charge.

Official Guide Book. See under Whithorn Priory.

Laggangairn Standing Stones

Two flat slabs marked with re-duplicated incised crosses of an early pattern.
Situation. At Kilgallioch, parish of New Luce. O.S. 1″ map sheet 79, ref. NX 222717.
Admission. All times without charge.

Monreith Cross

A notable free-standing wheel-headed cross with interlaced enrichment, 7 feet 6 inches high.
Situation. In the grounds of Monreith House about 1¾ miles south-east of Port William. O.S. 1″ map sheet 80, ref. NX 355429.
Admission. All reasonable times without charge.

Rispain Camp

A rectangular enclosure defined by double banks and ditches. Probably a medieval homestead site.
Situation. 1 mile west of Whithorn near Rispain Farm. O.S. 1″ map sheet 80, ref. NX 429399.
Admission. All times without charge.

St. Ninian's Cave

This cave is traditionally associated with the Saint who established the first Christian Church in Scotland in the early fifth century. It might well have been his place of retreat, as within there has been found a fine assemblage of early Christian crosses, now displayed in the museum attached to Whithorn Priory. Both upon the walls of the cave and the rocks outside Christian crosses have been incised at an early date and may be seen *in situ* behind protective grilles.
Situation. Physgill, on the coast 4 miles south-west of Whithorn. Footpath from Kidsdale Farm. O.S. 1″ map sheet 80, ref. NX 422360.
Admission. All times without charge.
Official Guide Book. Described in Whithorn Priory Guide Book, 2s.

St. Ninian's Chapel

The ruins of a chapel of thirteenth century date. Excavations have, failed to produce evidence of an earlier church. The chapel is a simple rectangle on plan. It had a doorway in the south wall, a pointed arched window in the north wall and a larger arched window in the east wall. The exterior is quite plain. The chapel stood within an enclosing wall, of which evidence is still visible. On the point of the promontory may be seen the earthworks of an Iron Age fort.
Situation. The Isle of Whithorn, about 5 miles south-east of Whithorn (A 750). O.S. 1″ map sheet 80, ref. NX 479362.
Admission. All times without charge.
Official Guide Book. Described in Whithorn Priory Guide Book. 2s.

Torhouse Stone Circle

A circle of 19 boulders standing on the edge of a low mound. Probably Bronze Age.

Situation. About 4 miles west of Wigtown and some 700 yards south-east of Torhousekie farm (B 733). O.S. 1″ map sheet 80, ref. NX 383565.
Admission. All times without charge.

★ *Whithorn Priory*

A church at Whithorn was founded by St. Ninian in the early fifth century, later dedicated to St. Martin. This was the first Christian church in Scotland. The medieval church was founded by Fergus, Lord of Galloway, in the twelfth century and became the cathedral church of Galloway, served by Premonstratensian canons regular. The ruins are scanty, but the chief feature of interest is the fine Norman doorway of the nave. In the museum are preserved a notable group of early Christian monuments, including the Latinus stone, dating from the fifth century, and the St. Peter Stone, showing a late form of the Christogram or Chi-Rho monogram.

Situation. At Whithorn. O.S. 1″ map sheet 80, ref. NX 445403.
Hours of Admission. Standard.
Admission Fee. 1s.
Official Guide Book. 2s. The Guide Book to Early Christian and Pictish Monuments of Scotland is also available. Price 5s.

The "Wren's Egg" Stone Circle

The remains of a standing stone circle, originally a double concentric ring. Only three stones remain, including the central one.

Situation. 2 miles south-east of Port William near the farmhouse of Blairbuie. O.S. 1″ map sheet 80, ref. NX 361420.
Admission. All times without charge.

PLATES

PLATES

Plate I. *The prehistoric village, Skara Brae, Orkney*

Plate 2. *Ring of Brogar, Stenness, Orkney*

Plate 3. *Stalled cairn, Midhowe, Orkney*

Plate 4. *Jarlshof, Shetland, from the air*
(By courtesy of Scotsman Publications Ltd.)

Plate 5. *Mousa Broch, Shetland*

Plate 6. *Meigle Museum, Perthshire*

Plate 7. *Sueno's Stone, Moray*

Plate 8. *St. Regulus' Church, St. Andrews, Fife*

Plate 9. *The Nave, Glasgow Cathedral*

Plate 10. *Crossraguel Abbey, Ayrshire*

Plate 11. *Dryburgh Abbey, Berwickshire*

Plate 12. *Melrose Abbey, Roxburghshire*

Plate 13. *Sweetheart Abley, Kirkcudbrightshire*

Plate 14. *Inchcolm Abbey, Fife*

Plate 15. *Linlithgow Palace, West Lothian*

Plate 16. *The east front, Elgin Cathedral, Moray*

Plate 17. *Dirleton Castle, East Lothian*

Plate 18. The great "donjon", Bothwell Castle, Lanarkshire

Plate 19. *Hermitage Castle, Roxburghshire*

Plate 20. *Tantallon Castle, East Lothian*

Plate 21. *Craigmillar Castle, Midlothian*

Plate 22. *Claypotts, Angus*

Plate 23. *The Gardens, Edzell Castle, Angus*

Plate 24. *Skelmorlie Aisle, Largs, Ayrshire*

FURTHER READING

General

Full descriptions of the monuments in the counties of Berwickshire; Caithness; Dumfries; East Lothian; Fife and Clackmannan; Galloway Vol. I: Wigtown, Vol. II: Kirkcudbright; Midlothian and West Lothian; Orkney and Shetland; Peebles; Roxburgh; Selkirkshire; Skye; Hebrides and Small Isles; Stirlingshire; Sutherland; City of Edinburgh will be found in the Inventories published under these titles by the Royal Commission on Ancient and Historical Monuments, Scotland.

Prehistoric Periods

PIGGOTT, S. and HENDERSON	1958	*Scotland Before History.*
CHILDE, V. G.	1934	*The Prehistory of Scotland.*
PIGGOTT, S. (Ed.)	1962	*Prehistoric Peoples of Scotland.*
FEACHEM, R.	1963	*Prehistoric Scotland.*
FEACHEM, R.	1966	*The North Britons.*
HENSHALL, A.	1965	*Chambered Tombs of Scotland,* I.
RIVET, A. L. F. (Ed.)	1967	*The Iron Age in North Britain.*

Roman Period

CRAWFORD, O. G. S.	1949	*The Topography of Roman Scotland.*
MACDONALD, G.	1934	*The Roman Wall in Scotland.*
ROBERTSON, A. S.	1960	*The Antonine Wall.*
SALWAY, P.	1965	*Frontier Peoples of Roman Britain.*
WILSON, D. R.	1967	*The Roman Frontiers of Britain.*
	1956	*O.S. Map of Roman Britain.*
RICHMOND, I. A. (Ed.)	1958	*Roman and Native in North Britain.*

Post-Roman Periods

CHADWICK, H. M.	1949	*Early Scotland.*
CRUDEN, S. H.	1957	*Early Christian and Pictish Monuments* (H.M.S.O.).
ALLEN, J. ROMILLY	1903	*Early Christian Monuments of Scotland.*
ANDERSON, J.	1881	*Scotland in Early Christian Times* (1881).
WAINWRIGHT, F. T. (Ed.)	1955	*Problem of the Picts.*
HENDERSON, I.	1967	*The Picts.*
MACGIBBON, D. and ROSS, T.	1887–92	*Castellated and Domestic Architecture of Scotland.*
MACGIBBON, D. and ROSS, T.	1896–7	*Ecclesiastical Architecture of Scotland.*
SIMPSON, W. D.	1943	*The Province of Mar.*
CRUDEN, S. H.	1960	*The Scottish Castle.*
CRUDEN, S. H.	1960	*Scottish Abbeys* (H.M.S.O.)
SIMPSON, W. D.	1959	*Scottish Castles* (H.M.S.O.)
MACKENZIE, W. M.	1927	*The Medieval Castle in Scotland.*
LINDSAY, I. G.	1960	*The Scottish Parish Kirk.*
DUNBAR, J. G.	1965	*Historic Architecture of Scotland.*

INDEX

Figures refer to the "Notes" only.

INDEX—*Continued*

INDEX—*Continued*

Ancient Monuments and
Historic Buildings

Many interesting ancient sites and buildings are maintained as national monuments by the Ministry of Public Building and Works. Guide-books, postcards and specially produced photographs are available as follows:

GUIDE-BOOKS or pamphlets are on sale at most monuments, and are also obtainable from the bookshops of Her Majesty's Stationery Office. A complete list of titles and prices is contained in Sectional List No. 27 available free on request from any of the addresses given on cover.

POSTCARDS can be purchased at many monuments, or from the Clerk of Stationery, Ministry of Public Building and Works, Argyle House, 3 Lady Lawson Street, Edinburgh, EH3 9SD (Clerk of Stationery, Ministry of Public Building and Works, Lafone House, 11/13 Leathermarket Street, London, S.E.1, for English and Welsh monuments).

OFFICIAL PHOTOGRAPHS of most monuments may be obtained in large prints (e.g. size $8\frac{1}{2}'' \times 6\frac{1}{2}''$; $10'' \times 8''$) at commercial rates from the Librarian, Ministry of Public Building and Works, Argyle House, 3 Lady Lawson Street, Edinburgh, EH3 9SD (Photographic Librarian, Ministry of Public Building and Works, Hannibal House, Elephant and Castle, London, S.E.1, for English and Welsh monuments).

SEASON TICKETS, valid for 12 months from date of issue, admitting their holders to all ancient monuments and historic buildings in the care of the Ministry, may be obtained from the Ministry or at many monuments.

Printed in Scotland by Her Majesty's Stationery Office Press, Edinburgh.
Dd. 239035 K280 (6233)